Holistic Freedom
A KinesioGeek Workbook

Ten Rules to Creating the Holistic Business of your dreams (and having fun doing it!)

By Alexis Costello

ISBN 978-0-9783865-1-1

Names have been changed to protect identities.

Colouring sheets are drawn by Dan Boyes and reprinted by permission, contact him at HQCosTheta@gmail.com

4   **Introduction**

        The Ten Rules:

7   **Rule One: Work it like a business**

17   **Rule Two: Consider the environment**

24   **Rule Three: It's not about you**

32   **Rule Four: It's all about relationships**

39   **Rule Five: Marketing is not a dirty word**

50   **Rule Six: Find your soapbox**

57   **Rule Seven: Walk the Talk**

65   **Rule Eight: Seeing is believing**

71   **Rule Nine: Seek out others**

76   **Rule Ten: Level up**

81   **Conclusion**

82   **Business Plan Template**

85   **Budget Template**

87   **Appendix 1**

87   **Appendix 2**

89   **KinesioGeek Manifesto**

90   **Core Values List**

INTRODUCTION

We need to ask a better question.

The old question is: "Would you do it if you didn't need the money?"

That's the question they always tell you to ask isn't it? If you won the lottery, what would you do? And the answer is supposed to show you your passion, help you 'find your bliss' and know what path you want to follow. Here's the thing, I know the answer is yes – I would do energy work and muscle testing if I didn't need the money. Absolutely. But the flip side of it is that I have never, ever, had that luxury. For me, this has never been a hobby or a chance at personal development or self-healing (though of course those things have happened in the process), it has been a job. Yes it's a calling, yes it is good for the world, but it has also been how I put food on the table for my kids and pay the mortgage. If you want it to do that for you too; if you are interested in a modality of holistic health as a career, then this is for you.

> Here's a new question:
> What's the change you want to make?

And if you want to do it in a way that is true to your values, feels genuine and makes you sparkle, then we are going to get along just fine.

There is value to the old question – remember, clichés become clichés because they work. And everything I said in the above paragraph is true. But here's a new question: "What is the change you want to make?"

Well that's a whole different story isn't it.

Many of us start in the natural health field because we want to help people, but too often practitioners get discouraged along the way. Or, even worse, they lose track of why they are here in the first place. If we can focus on making a change, then it will help when things feel daunting, give us courage in the face of obstacles, and remind us of the love that brought us here in the beginning. If these words resonate with you; if you want to make a big change in the world, but also need this to be a business then you are in a powerful position. This workbook will help you to clarify your vision, figure out exactly what change you wish to make and who it will affect. Best of all, it will give you the tools to help you get there.

A few years ago, I put together the GEMS Flow and Business classes (with some help from my mom, one of the most amazing practitioners I have ever had the opportunity to work with) because I could see that my students were struggling. They had taken classes in

Touch for Health and some of them had other modalities as well. They had tools that they wanted to share with the world, and yet, they seemed unable to get going with a business. So, they end up broke and bitter, or they have to spend all of their time working their day job and end up too tired to do much with this new crazy field they have fallen in love with, so it gets pushed aside and hardly used. Maybe you see yourself in one of these categories? The world needs every one of these practitioners; but we need to have a better game plan if we want a larger portion of those who start in the field to end up feeling successful and not lose half of them along the way.

I have been working in the holistic health field for a long time, mostly in the role of a practitioner. When I began working with muscle-testing I was in a well-established centre that employed other practitioners as sub-contractors too. It was a fantastic place to start because it let me learn from a variety of people who had been doing this for a lot longer than me. I was able to hone my skills without too much risk. I had another job at a health food store that I gradually was working less and less at as I gained more clients, but I still remember how terrifying it was to take the final leap and leave my 'real' job. Years later I left the health centre , my clients and the world I knew to spend 6 months tromping through Costa Rica with my family studying herbs in the rainforest. When we returned, I knew I wanted to do things differently than what I had been doing at the centre, which had an entrenched and established set of procedures; so I started up my own place. Now I live in Costa Rica, attempting to create a more self-sufficient lifestyle with my family, but I still spend about half of my year traveling and teaching. When I sold my business, I realized that I was making a big shift in what I felt like I wanted to do. While I still see clients, (and can honestly not imagine a world in which I don't work on people) my focus has changed. I understand that my role now is to train and support other practitioners and instructors, and that is where this workbook is coming from. Yes, I want to work on people, but I'm so small, I know that the world needs more than I can offer it. But if I can help others get to where they want to be, then we will truly change the world together. Does that sound idealistic? Perhaps. But the point of the Big Why is that it is supposed to be something bigger than you. Dream big or go home.

This is not a how-to muscle test book; I couldn't improve upon what is already available, there are amazing classes out there that will teach you how to test muscles, procedures and protocols, and some of these are listed in the appendices at the back along with how to find an instructor in your area. This assumes that you already have a certain skill set under your belt in your chosen field, but that maybe you are interested in the so-called 'soft skills'. I know many massage practitioners, Reiki masters, Registered Holistic Nutritionists and Touch for Health instructors that are having trouble meeting their financial goals or making the shift from part-time working on friends and family to this being their 'real' job. These are some thoughts about how to set up a business that resonates with your clients, how to build a network in a genuine way, why the natural health field is important and how to share that message with the public, as well as ideas about where we are going in the future.

When I have spoken with people in the past about my intention to put out a book like this into the world to help struggling practitioners (or just those who want to up their game), I have been asked 'why?'. Why train the competition? Isn't it better to stay a step ahead and let others flounder? And this is the kind of thinking that the old business models propagate – the idea that there is only so much to go around and if you have a slice then there is less for me. If you believe that the world needs more holistic practitioners, then you want to help this come about. There are about seven billion people in the world. I think it's safe to say that all of them could use some stress management or body work in one aspect or another. How many of them are you going to see as clients? Is it less than 1000? Do you think there might be room to share? I want other practitioners to do well so that we can, as a unit, help more people. I want them to do well, so that, when I am sick or in pain, I can find skilled people to help me feel better. I want others to do well, so that when I tell people what I do for a living, they have at least heard if it before, as every credible, successful practitioner out there raises the awareness and viability of our field. Everything we can do that makes our field more visible to the general public in a positive way is a good thing that will help us all to be more successful in the end. This idea that we need to compete with each other in order to rise to the top is part of an old and mostly dead paradigm – we are interested in something new.

This book outlines a series of Rules for pushing your holistic business ahead. Feeling a little rebellious at the thought of 'rules'? OK, *guidelines* then. Suggestions. Ideas. For each one I will bat the concept around a little, tell you a few stories and then lay out an Action Plan. These are meant to be things that you can take and put into practice right away, so that, as soon as you begin working with the book, you are able to begin doing things that help you move ahead in your business, make meaningful connections with your clients, and feel more confident about your strategy.

Book bonus features:

By now hopefully you have realized that this is not meant to be a book that you will read and then put away. This is a workspace. Along with the Action Plan at the end of each section you will also find an affirmation card. These can be cut out and posted around the house as a reminder of goals that you are working on as you explore the text. Or photocopied. Or take a photo with your phone and share it. Or, depending on the type of holistic therapy that you work with, they may become goals for balances and sessions, allowing you to see where you might have stress on the idea and diffuse it, making progress possible at an accelerated rate. Or maybe you will simply fold them into paper airplanes and throw them at the people you love. Whatever helps you out. The truth of the matter is, I hope you destroy this book. I hope it is full of notes and ideas and you writing out your thoughts for the Action items and checking them off and diving in again with new goals as your business shifts and changes and grows. I hope you enjoy the colouring pages and find them therapeutic. I hope you love it so much that you want to track me down online to tell me about it, and if you hate it (or some aspect of it), I want to hear that too (though admittedly less than I want to hear the good stuff. Let's be honest here). In the spirit of helping each other become better.

Be amazing, and let's do what we can to kick this whole industry up a notch, shall we?

RULE #1: WORK IT LIKE A BUSINESS

It sounds cold blooded, to talk about the healing arts as a business. But that is what this book is about. And yet, not in the most traditional of ways; many books on business and creating your own business especially have a sort of bombastic 'sell sell sell!' kind of refrain to them. They have an underlying message that seems to say that you are smarter and work harder than everyone else and that is why you are going to rise to the top over all the lazy drones that are not clever enough to read said book. Like so many of you, I am sick of re-reading versions of that book published again and again by different authors. Again, we need to be asking different questions; we need to create change.

I am assuming that if you have landed here, you already understand how and why working with the body in a natural and holistic way is important. For myself, I don't just believe that Specialized Kinesiology is a job, I believe it is a calling, a way of life, a way of making the world a better place and those are the reasons why I do what I do. But when we switch from talking about *why* we work in this field to *how* we are working in it, then we need to discuss it like a business.

Let's be clear though, this is holistic business, and there is a huge and definable difference. When we talk about holistic business, what we mean is business that comes from the heart. That is not at the expense of family, friends and personal care, but is driven forward by them. In this case the word 'holistic' is defining not the skill set (as in, I work with essential oils, or massage or some other 'alternative health' modality) but rather the way it is being done – that this is something that touches every aspect of your life. That you are coming at it from a place of love and authenticity. The love is what gives energy to the cells, it is what focuses the intention, it's what provides the motivation. If it

"It has to come from a place of love

It's what focuses the energy.
It's what fuels the cells.
It's what makes the difference.
Otherwise you're just pushing buttons."

www.alexiscostello.com

doesn't come from a place of love than all you are doing is pushing buttons. The love and intention is the reason why the best massage chair in the world, with all the fancy rollers and robotics will never replace going for good bodywork. It is the secret sauce. And it may seem like I am harping on this, but that's because I want to make it crystal clear, right here in the beginning – you can follow all of the steps, write the plans and do the work, but if your heart's not in it and you don't have the right motivation, it shows.

If you are the kind of person who naturally gravitates to this holistic business model, then you may find yourself repelled by the idea of being a business owner, of managing people, or marketing, as these ideas might all have negative connotations in your head. When I say that we are discussing it like a business, what I mean is that we need to focus for awhile on some of the aspects of planning and practice that might not come easily to all of us. Most of the people who find themselves drawn to this type of work will not have had formal business or management training. We tend to be kinesthetic people who like to get their hands into stuff and don't necessarily thrive in the typical university classroom. We are 'people people', the type who want to help others rather than crunch numbers. I hear you; there is no amount of brain integration work that is going to get me excited about account-ing or relaxed in the face of my long-overdue taxes. There are exceptions to this as with all things of course, but this seems to be true for the majority of practitioners I have met.

There are great books that you can read to help you think like a business person. But better yet, there are books that have come out in the past twenty years or so that break the mold of the books I mentioned earlier. Books by authors who understand that in this world of hyper-connectivity, business and art are not mutually exclusive, in fact the more creativity, people skills, originality and authenticity you can bring into your business the better!

> Because of the informal nature of both training and work in the holistic health field, there is less definition between student and practitioner.

If you were going to open up a storefront, there are usually certain steps that you would go through. You might look up the kind of business you want to open and see what kind of competition is in your area and how they price their services. You would write up a business plan and figure out a budget so that you know what your store will cost you every month in terms of rent, utilities, stock, etc. You might invest in some good accounting software to help you keep track of your sales and inventory and maybe hire a bookkeeper or accountant to keep things in check. You would think about marketing and advertising and set up a budget to get the word out about what you do so that your customers can find you. These are normal activities for someone opening up a corner store, but for some reason, almost unheard of in the holistic health industry.

What happens with health practitioners usually follows a trajectory more like this: you are seeing a practitioner and you find what they do really interesting. Eventually you do some reading and decide to take a class. You love the class and begin working on your friends and family in the evening or a weekend. You fantasize about the day you can quit your day job and do this work full time, but have no idea how to go about it. This state of affairs continues until you either a) jump in, maybe a little unprepared, but trying to make a go of it anyways with varying results, or b) lose the enthusiasm you had for your modality and feel like it is impossible. It is very rare for people to be able to make the transition gracefully without any help.

Because of the informal nature of both training and work in the holistic health field, there is less definition between student and practitioner. This is not true in all countries, for example, Australia and many European countries have specific guidelines about the amount of training required in an accredited school before you are recognized officially as a facilitator in a specific modality and are therefore allowed to work professionally. In North America however, this isn't the case. Much of our work is unrecognized, and we use a variety of terminology that can mean different things in different areas. This means that there can be a huge gulf in the amount of training that various practitioners have, which can be confusing for someone looking to make an appointment with someone for the first time. Many courses expect students to do case studies where they work on a certain number of people to acquire proficiency. Some modalities have guidelines about how many classes or free case studies you should do before you hang out your shingle, but others have no set guidelines at all. When I began taking Touch for Health classes, I knew I was smitten. I was already certified in herbology, iridology, aromatherapy, etc. but this was what I had been waiting for. I was already working in an office using some of the aforementioned skills so I had a few clients already. I took my level one weekend Touch for Health class, walked into work Monday morning and told my clients that I had learned something new on the weekend that I wanted to try out on them. A classic example of me jumping into something head-first without really having any clue what I'm doing. This kind of approach has pros and cons obviously. On the upside, it prevents 'analysis paralysis' as you just dive in before you have a chance to become self-conscious about what you don't know. The con of course, is that you really don't know very much, so it can be kind of embarrassing in the future when you look back and realize how little you knew when you worked on a particular client.

> Once you make the decision that you want this to be your real job, you need to treat it as such.

The informality of this type of education is brilliant in many ways. It allows people to try out something new with a relatively small outlay of time and money (compared with say, enrolling in a college or university program). It allows for gradual transitions as someone begins to see more clients and gains confidence in a skill set. But these blurred lines do not lend themselves to things like business plans, and that's where there is some room for improvement.

Once you make the decision that you want this to be your real job, you need to treat it as such. Find the Community Futures office or equivalent in your area that offers help and guidance for local small business. They often have information about bylaws or things to consider specific to your region and can offer advice and help to people starting out. I have included a template for a basic business plan and budget at the back of this book – you can start working on it as soon as possible and then can add to it as you go through this workbook and begin considering different aspects. There is also a template that you can download from the gemskinesiology.com website so that you can work on your business plan on a computer, but I suggest that you try it with a pen the first time. Your brain works differently when you have a pen or pencil in hand rather than a keyboard and we tend to be more creative and have better access to the gestalt side of the brain when in this pose (for more thoughts about this, check out the book Steal Like an Artist in the   appendix in the back). You can simply make notes in this book, then type out a proper draft afterwards from the ideas you have jotted down if you like. Working on a proper business plan will help you think clearly about what you are offering to the community and how it is similar and different than what is already out there. It will help you to reflect back on that original question; what is the change you are hoping to make?

In order to put together a business plan and a budget projection, you will need to think realistically about how many clients you can see in a week. This has a few components to it; how many hours a day do you want to work is important sure, but also what will your community support? There is a huge variance in acceptance of alternative therapies in different areas. When I first started working in this field in 2003, we were living in a small town in Northern Saskatchewan. I wrote a weekly column about health and nutrition for the local paper (a gig I got by offering to do it for free) and the paper actually received hate mail from people extremely upset that I had suggested that perhaps people would be better off eating a little less meat, dairy and wheat. I can only imagine what would have happened if I had dared to discuss something like chakras, auric fields, or how to access the subconscious through muscle testing. In that community, at that time, it would have been impossible to make a proper career out of alternative health, which was a major factor in our decision to move to a different province. Though I am a fervent believer in the idea that holistic health is really for everyone, we just need to find the right way to offer it to them; in some places this is going to be easier than others. At that time, seeing two or three clients a week was all I was managing, but now it would be an entirely different story.

A good business plan will include some hard conversations about money. When I teach the GEMS Business class, money always comes up as something that creates blocks for practitioners; whether it's a question of how much to charge or how to go about collecting it for a session. Because we are dealing with health and emotions and issues that can be extremely sensitive, it can be difficult to then turn around and ask someone to pay you. But in order for this to become your true business you need to. If you were selling a product, you wouldn't hesitate to ask people to pay for it. That being said, there are always exceptions and I know I have given away a lot of sessions over the years, either because I knew someone needed help and genuinely couldn't afford it or as a 'thank you' for someone's loyalty or referrals, or just in the form of gift certificates for school fund raisers or charity events. But for the average person, paying for a session actually seems to benefit them more that getting it for free. Think of it like a gym membership for a moment. If someone is given a free gym membership, they are much less likely to use it than someone who is paying for it every single month. On the mornings when it's cold and you're tired, you are much more likely to haul your aching body out of bed and go to spin class if you already paid for it than if you haven't invested anything. I find that in general, clients who are paying you for your time are much more likely to take your

> *The Business Plan Template is at the back of the book—check out page 82 to get started*

suggestions to heart and make the lifestyle changes that may be needed in order to promote good health.

A few guidelines about pricing:

Never compete on price. All the business books agree on this – you don't want to be the one people choose because you are the cheapest; someone is always going to be willing to do it for less. I learned this for myself the one time I agreed to do a Groupon-style coupon for my office. It was a local chapter run by someone in a women-in-business group that I used to meet with, and I agreed to do the promotion in order to support her. We created a promotion for discounted massages, since bio-energetic muscle testing is a much more difficult thing to explain to people in the kind of short blurb space you are given with this kind of promo. Here's the thing; I know we gave ridiculously good massages at our office. We had a die-hard fan base that had been booking regularly for years. But none of the people who came in with the coupons became regulars. Not one. Once the discount was used, they moved on to the next discounted service (I assume). I would never do that again.

Price your services according to the way you wish to be working and the group that you are trying to serve. I have always worked extensively with children and teenagers and their families. I usually wanted to see them every three or four weeks for the first few months in order to get them on track. If people are going to be coming to see you regularly, you need to set your prices differently than 'luxury' sessions, like those found in a destination spa for instances. If you want to be part of someone's regular family expenses, then you need to price in such a way that this is feasible. If you, like some of my peers, want to only work with high-level athletes, then you price differently as they obviously have a different budget set up for personal care than a mom of three does. Understand your target market and what is doable for them. It can be helpful to look online and see what people are charging for similar services in your area and then place yourself appropriately in the spectrum.

Remember that it is a balancing act and that you always have a choice in how you proceed from here. You are allowed to make exceptions for people; to offer discounts or freebies to regulars or someone having a tough time. I know that I price my sessions a little lower than many in my industry. Occasionally I get a little flak from someone; "Don't you think you're worth more than that?" "I need to charge more than that to balance out my education." Hey, I'm not judging you. And my self-worth is not tied to the amount that I charge for sessions, so I don't need to compete here. I have heard people get into conversations about how much they charge where there seems to be an assumption in place that the person who commands the most money for their sessions is the best. This is not true. The most expensive session is not the best, the cheapest session is not always the worst, the two are not actually tied to each other. Figure out what you are comfortable with and don't worry about what anyone else thinks about that. This is one of those 'to each his own' things, and we are probably all better off coming up with numbers that make sense for us personally rather than trying to make everyone in your area come to a consensus.

Whatever you decide about pricing, make sure it is clearly visible to people visiting your office and your website so there are no surprises. If you tend to be a little on the passive-aggressive side (and really, how many of us aren't?) rather than directly asking for payment ("That will be $75 please.") you can offer a choice ("Would you prefer to use a debit card or pay cash today?"). Remember that your attitude sets the tone for this trans-action; if you are hesitant or awkward about it, the client can pick up on that and might be too. If you are clear and confident about it as just the normal next step in the session, they will follow suit.

One aspect that is not usually included on a traditional business plan but certainly should be, is to look at core values. Take a look at the list on pages__ in the appendix. Feel free to circle as many of these words as appeal to you (it's weirdly satisfying isn't it?), but under-stand that, in the end, what we are looking for are 2 or 3 core values, ideally with one that rises to the surface as the most important value for you in business. This is it. This is the beginning of your branding because if everything you put out there to the public goes back to this core idea then 1) you will feel confident and joyful about everything you say, 2) it will be genuine and authentic, and people can sense that. You will never be the greasy car-salesman, 3) it gives you a filter to look at marketing materials through. If your core value is 'perfection' you are going to market very differently than someone whose core value is 'empathy'. The art, the language, everything would reflect either one value or the other and people will get a very different feeling from one or the other and both are good and will attract different people. It is too easy for us in the natural health field to settle on words like 'holistic', 'natural' and 'helping'. These things are true of course and there is a place for them in your material. But what is better at this point is to assume that those words are a given, because they are the common ground that we are all building on. What you want to focus on here is what makes you unique. What makes you different than every other health practitioner out there? And when we underline and highlight those little differences, we allow our personality to shine through and are better able to connect with those that we are trying to reach.

The real test of this though is to test-drive saying it. Put it out somewhere in the world; tell a friend or post it online – let people know what you have come up with. You'll know that it's right if it feels a tiny bit scary or vulnerable to say it out loud, but also makes you feel good; that's what we're looking for.

At this point you have a list of amazing words that you feel describe you and your business; but how do we decide which one(s) are the key? You can begin by asking yourself a few questions. For example, what would you consider to be your best qualities? What qualities and values do you admire in others and strive to emulate? What qualities really bother you in yourself and in those around you? How do you want people to describe you?

I have done this at a few conferences with groups of holistic health practitioners now and it is always interesting. Those of us who muscle test are notorious cheats with this kind of game because we often will just muscle test the list. This is easier in some ways, but also means that it is possible to be surprised by what comes up. When you say your core words to people who know you though, they shouldn't be surprised. Jeff Bezos is often quoted as saying that, "Personal Brand is what people say about you when you leave the room." This means that you already have a personal brand, whether you like it or not. And it may or may not be flattering or be the message that you would ultimately like to see conveyed. If you're curious about what the public perception of you and your work is, you can ask your friends. Ask people for 3 words that best describe you or describe the experience of having a session with you, and then see what words start coming up consistently.

This can give you a jumping off point – if you don't like the words that you are hearing, then you can do something about it.

Don't toss the other words from the list because together they tell a story about you and there will be a place for each of these values in your business, just remember that one of them is the key. Once you know what is most important to you in your work-life, it is easier to begin marketing and branding – one of the most overlooked facets of our industry as a whole.

This idea of working with your value words is going to come back over and over through-out this workbook. You will need these words to help you find the perfect environment, create your avatar, get into your marketing strategy, so don't skip this bit.

Action Plan:

1) Take a look at the Business Plan template at the back of this book. Expect to spend several hours working with this in order to do it properly, though these hours don't have to be all at once. Begin now and add to it as you define your business while going through this workbook. Think of this process as an organic work in progress – it is ok for it to evolve and change, so don't worry if you don't feel like you have the perfect answers yet; the trick is just to get started.

If you want something a little more official to work with than what I have created for you here, it is easy to find templates online. Here is a link to the page sponsored by the Canadian Government for small businesses: https://canadabusiness.ca/business-planning/sample-business-plans-and-templates/

And from the Business Development Center: https://www.bdc.ca/en/articles-tools/entrepreneur-toolkit/templates-business-guides/pages/business-plan-template.aspx

And Inc.com has a Top Ten Business plans that you can download for free page here: https://www.inc.com/larry-kim/top-10-business-plan-templates-you-can-download-free.html

(All these links are available for you on gemskinesiology.com if you don't want to type them in)

2) Think about what you are going to charge for your sessions. Find at least five practitioners in your area who work with various modalities and research what they charge. Practice telling people what you charge for a session and make sure that you are comfortable with the number you are saying; that it doesn't feel ridiculously high or low for you.

The most expensive sessions in my area are $_____ offered by _____

The least expensive sessions in my area are $_____ offered by _____

Here are some numbers I feel comfortable with to start:

3) Go through the hundreds of words at the back of the book starting on page 90 and find your key values. Don't over think it. This first round can just be about circling everything that appeals to you and then you can begin to rate them until you figure out what is most important.

4) To finish off the Core Values exercise, find someone whose opinion you value and tell them the words that you have come up with. Ask them if the words seem like a good fit. And if this is someone you know well and they seem to be genuinely puzzled as to why your would choose these words, then you can reevaluate.

Want to write them down here?

"I create the holistic business of my dreams."

"My business is perfectly aligned with my core values."

RULE ONE: WORK IT LIKE A BUSINESS

Kinesiogeek:
Someone who genuinely believes that an understanding of muscle testing might just save the world.

WWW.ALEXISCOSTELLO.COM

RULE # 2: CONSIDER THE ENVIRONMENT

Some of the most-watched television and best-selling books of the past year have been about how to clean up and declutter your space. People are paying attention because they have realized that your environment has a huge influence over your health, your emotions and your productivity. Do not underestimate the importance of being comfortable in your surroundings. Create the space that is going to work best for you.

When I started my office all those years ago, I had a distinct idea of how I wanted the space to feel. I had a vision of a space that felt so comfortable, healing and friendly that people would want to be there – that it would be an enjoyable space simply to wait around in. This worked extremely well. We would often hear things from our clients like, "I feel better as soon as I come in here", "It always smells so good in here". People would show up early for a cup of tea and linger after their appointments were finished. The space we choose for our business sets the tone for the entire experience. If you want people to come back again and again, you need to create a space they want to return to; a space that speaks to them in some deep way. This is something that the top brands in the world know about and leverage. The clean sparse interior of an Apple store or the luxurious opium-den decor of a spa; design changes the way people feel in a space and also what they are willing to pay for the experience. I am willing to pay more for a decadent experience in a beautiful place where I feel transported from my everyday life than I am for a great appointment in someone's basement. Packaging matters. If you want to completely seduce your new clients until they can't imagine going anywhere else, you need to create an environment that they crave. This is not the same across the board, what appears on a visceral level to one person is off-putting to another, the trick is to figure out what the group you want to work with is looking for and go after specifically that, not to try to please all people (a marketing recipe for disaster).

Look at the list of adjectives on the next page. If you had to pick just a couple, how would you want your clients to describe your space? Try to pick things that go along with your brand.

At the back of this book is a huge list of adjectives that you can begin working with to figure out your core values and branding, this is just a tiny sample. Feel free to flip there now and start playing with it if you like! If you have already done the Core Values exercise, then you want to make sure that the look and feel of your space is congruent with what you have already decided on.

For example, my tagline on my website is 'Because Health should be fun!" therefore my office spaces tend to be bright with whimsical art and punches of colour. I like to have

NATURAL   cooperative

expensive

homey PROFESSIONAL

fun

sterile   *pampering*

family-friendly MEDICAL

comforting relaxing

water with fruit in it and herbal tea and maybe some cookies that I made the night before kicking around. There are toys and books in a bin in the corner (since I work with so many young families), comfy chairs to flop into and interesting things to read. In my old office, if you walked in on any given day when my youngest was a baby, you might have seen me at the front desk nursing, or when he was a little bigger, playing with bottles of supplements and pushing them around the floor while I priced them. It was fun, relaxed and comfortable. To another practitioner, this is a vision of unprofessional Hell. For me, and many of my clients, it was Paradise.

Because of the nature of my work now, I no longer have this kind of designated space. When people come to my glorified treehouse for a session, I have a table overlooking the jungle with the river rushing in the background and there is a good chance I will have to chase a chicken out at some point. It is not perfect, but it reflects my life here. It is definitely genuine...

Your office space will often be the first glimpse someone has of you and the kind of work that you do. Just like you want your business card to be an accurate reflection of the spirit of your work, your workspace should feel 'right' for who you are and what you do.

We need to think about more than brand congruency though. For example, what do you need to have at hand in order to make this the experience that you want for your clients? Whatever manuals, technology, crystals, tuning forks, flower essences, etc. that you are going to need in order to give a great session, these things need to be readily available so that you don't waste your client's time by having to leave the room to search for things as you go. Having your tools on hand will help you to look and feel more professional.

At the beginning, you may decide that you just want to work with clients out of your home rather than investing in office space. There isn't anything wrong with this, but there might be legalities to consider depending on the bylaws of the area where you live. Some places have strict rules about the type of commercial activities that can be carried out, or there might be rules about parking, hours of operation, insurance required, etc. When viewing the Action Plan at the end of this chapter, pay attention to the item regarding compliance to these rules so you don't find yourself in trouble before you even get off the ground.

If you want to create the perfect environment, consider that this involves more than just the things that make up the environment; it also encompasses your relationship to them.

For example, a table is just a table. But for one person, it is the place where they write, pay bills and browse Facebook, whereas for another person it might be the formal dinning room set that is only used on special occasions for family dinners. The exact items that make up the environment matter much less than how we use them and the habits that we form in relation to them. If you create an environment that is conducive to the habits that you want to cultivate, eventually you get to the point where you don't have to use will-power in order to make yourself do something – all you do is put yourself in the correct environment and the behavior seems to take care of itself.

Willpower is tricky. There have been studies that suggest that it is a finite thing and show that you have an easier time sticking to a diet in the morning rather than the evening, for example. And yet there are other studies that seem to show that it is your belief in your own willpower that makes the difference. If you are like me, you might have a ridiculous number of things that you want to do with your day (like, a pathologically ridiculous number of things) and you have several lofty ideas about what you will get done in the limited time you have. Anything that you can do to help make it easier for yourself to get things done is a good thing. This seems so obvious and yet, many of us are resistant to creating good work habits.

The idea of creating habits through environmental cues is important because so many of the holistic health students that I work with lament the fact that they can't seem to make time to study or that they can't seem to get any practice sessions in; but what would happen if they set up an environment that was dedicated to such things? So that they know, deep in their subconscious mind, that when they step into the office space on a Sunday afternoon with a cup of tea, that it is time to study? That when they bring out certain books and charts it is a signal to their brain that it is time to work?

Many of us in the kinesiology world work with hand or finger modes. The idea behind this, if it's a concept that you are not familiar with, is that, when you place your hands in certain positions, you are creating specific frequencies (this is based on the mudras created in Ayurvedic medicine thousands of years ago) and those frequencies then allow you to define where you are going with your muscle testing. For example, many acupoints are used over and over again in different modalities to different effect – adding a specific hand-mode creates the context, so that I know what precisely the point means at his moment in time. Students in my classes have probably heard me say 100 times that, in kinesiology, context is everything. To my way of thinking, we should be able to do the same thing with our environment, creating context for our own actions that make it easier for us to operate at peak performance. We are creatures of habit, so make them productive ones. In the morning, at the same(ish) time every morning, I bring my phone with my language learning apps to a specific place in my yard, sit down and do my lessons. You have to work at this for the first couple of weeks, but after that, it becomes second nature for me to look at the clock, shut down whatever I was doing on my computer and go do a language lesson. Once you set up the habit, it takes the cognitive load off – it is no longer something that you need to think about or remember, it will happen automatically.

Timing within sessions can become a habit too. I have been doing hour-long sessions for so long that my body is tuned to that rhythm and, even without a clock in the room, my sessions are very consistent in length. The rhythm and flow of a session can be part of setting the environment. Many practitioners have a hard time staying within their allotted appointment spaces and it is usually because of their own love for their clients and the work – they just want to do as much as is physically possible before sending the individual they are working with back out into the real world! And yet, sticking to your time is a mark of the professional. And while your clients might appreciate the extra time you devote to them, they might also have something scheduled immediately after their time with you and be stressed if they can't leave when they had anticipated.

Like everything else, this requires discretion and flexibility depending on the situation. There are going to be sessions when you really need a little more time. There will be days when you are unavoidably late. And yet, you don't want this to be part of your reputation or brand – you're a professional, and pros know how to set the tone. Decide how long you want your sessions to be and how much time you need between them in order to best serve yourself and your target demographic and then put it into your business plan.

It is obvious that it is useful to create some good habits in life, but it might be less obvious why this is in a business plan and start-up book. It is simply this; you need to create a habit of doing the work. Yes, this is harder if you don't actually have many clients yet, but you need to set up the habit anyways. Create the context. Set up the space. If you are brand new and not in a position to go buy or rent office space yet while you are working out of your living room, that's ok. Find a couple of props that signal to your mind that it is time to work now. Bring out your books, your charts, your Enya CDs, whatever, and make it into an office space. The message to your subconscious is, when these things are here, this is not the space where we binge watch Netflix and eat pizza, this is the space where we work. Decide what day of the week is going to be your office day, set up your space, and then be in that space. If you don't have paying clients yet, invite friends over to be case studies. Invite a fellow student over for a practice. Sit and study your material. Balance yourself. Anything to begin creating a habit that says; this is my space, this is my work, it is important and I am making time for it regularly. After awhile, you won't have to think about it. If you build it, they will come.

But only if you are actually there and doing something worthwhile.

Action plan:

1) Visit 4 or 5 of your favourite places and write don't a few notes about the ambiance. What colours are they using? How does it smell? What is the overall feel or vibe that you get from the décor? Are there any common denominators that you can incorporate in your own design?

Notes:

_____

_____

_____
_____
_____
_____
_____
_____
_____
_____
_____

2) Consider your options for office space. In your area, does it make more sense to rent or buy? Do you want to work with a team in a shared space or are you more of a lone wolf? Consider things like bathroom location, cleanliness, noise level and what areas people will walk through before getting to your office space.

Thoughts:

_____
_____
_____
_____

3) If you are going to be setting up a home office you may need to look into the bylaws in your area to find out whether or not you are permitted to have a home business. There may be rules about parking, how many people you can have there at any given time, etc. Most cities have an official website where you can find these; simply Google your city name and bylaws, at which point you should be able to find what you need for your neighbourhood.

4) Create a space to work in and bring in sensory cues to train your mind to get ready for the work ahead. Do it daily/weekly, whatever fits the dream schedule you are trying to create for yourself.

"My environment suits and supports me perfectly."

"This space is filled with_____"
(fill in your blank)

RULE TWO: CONSIDER THE ENVIRONMENT

RULE # 3: IT'S NOT ABOUT YOU

And it's not about me. It's easy to develop a serious ego in this line of work. Because of the specificity that can come up when you are working deeply with your clients, people begin to attribute all kinds of super powers to you. I get questions all the time along the lines of, "When did you first realize you were psychic?" or statements like, "You healed my (fill in the blank) completely!" It is important to understand that it's not me that heals anything; it has nothing to do with me. This is not false modesty, it is an understanding of the way that muscle testing works and the information that can be found therein if you know how to look for it. And all healing comes from within. As Andrew Weil would say, a 'Healer' is someone who was sick and became well. A 'Great Healer' is someone who got sick and became well quickly.

We know this as practitioners because it is drummed into our heads when we begin taking kinesiology classes, particularly if you begin with the Touch for Health synthesis which emphasizes the Self Responsibility Model and the idea that it is always about the client. And yet. I'm sure it has happened to me before – you receive a glowing letter of thanks from a client about how you cured their pain/injury/disease and before too long you begin thinking that you're pretty great and that all anyone needs is to come have a session and listen to what you have to say. If this happens to you, don't worry; you will have a terrible session that will undo the damage soon enough.

In Steven Pressfield's business cult classic 'The War of Art' he makes the case that one of the consummate differences between the amateur and the professional is that the professional understands while doing her work, that it is not about her in the end. That she allows the Muse to come through her but understands that this is a source above and beyond or outside of her. This understanding allows for some professional detachment, rather than clinging to how the work is received.

Occasionally in the health field this indulgence of ego takes another sneakier form. When I first started working on clients, I worked at an office with several other practitioners under a wonderful guru-type. She was great with her clients and a generous and thoughtful instructor. On a personal level however, she struggled with her weight. One of the first things she said to me when I began working there (and to my mother as well, who worked in the same office, but started a year before me) was that I would gain at least 30lbs in next six months or so. She had a belief system that said that practitioners store energetic junk from their clients, and thought that level of energetic junk would cause the body to create layers of protection.

I don't think so.

Yes, taking on stress or baggage from others is an issue for some people, but it is one that can be overcome. In others, it begins to almost take the form of a conceit: "I'm so sensitive, I'm an empath, I take on everyone's energy!" The belief here is that your sensitivity makes you special. And it might. Empathy and the ability to feel strongly for others is helpful in many situations, but when it begins to get in the way of your ability to do your job properly, then it stops being a superpower and begins to look more like a liability. At that point, it is no longer cause for bragging (or fake-complaining) or celebration, it is something that needs to be turned down a notch so you can do what needs to be done.

Have I offended you here? If you see yourself in the words above, you have probably also had the experience of feeling absolutely drained after a few clients or getting sick because you have given too much of yourself away. If you are happy with the way things are and with the role that you are capable of in the health of others, then this is fine. But if you are hoping to be able to do more, then something has to give. In some cases, people who could be practitioners find that they have the same experience time and again; as soon as they begin working with others, they get overwhelmed or sick. If this is happening to you, I would strongly recommend 'The War of Art' as mentioned above, as it will help you to see the role of The Resistance and how it is keeping you from shining the way that you could. We could also do a session around the issue to clear the emotional blockages, but that might just be my own ego talking...

> *Have I offended you here?*
>
> *If you are hoping to be able to do more, then something's*
>
> *got to give.*

When we understand clearly that it's not about us as practitioners, this becomes less of a problem. I don't "take on my client's stuff" in session because that's not my job. My job is to allow them to come apart where they need to in order to let go of the old patterns and such that are not serving them anymore and they can't do that if they are afraid of hurting me or if I'm breaking down alongside them. This is something that needs to be balanced with what I have said before about authenticity. Because, let's face it, there are days when your 'authentic self' feels like something the cat dragged in. There are days when you know you are in rough shape; when you are going through emotional stress or you are tired, or something else is very wrong in your life. The difference between the professional and the amateur at this point is that the pro doesn't let it show. Be yourself, be authentic, be honest, but you also need to step up and do what needs to be done, even if you are upset or triggered by what is happening with your client at the moment.

This chapter has to be in here because I think in every class I have ever taught, at some point a student asks me how I protect or shield myself from the energy-craziness when I am working. I know practitioners that have developed long and involved rituals for such things, but I like to keep it simple when I'm in session, so here are a few ideas.

1) Understand that the more grounded and balanced you are, the less you are affected by other people's energy in general. Therefore, taking a moment to switch

on or give yourself a quickie balance before you start a work day can do wonders for you. If you find that you are being triggered by a certain client, make a note of it and get a session with a Holistic Health Professional friend whom you trust and figure out why this is such a big issue for you. If you continue to be triggered by this individual afterwards, refer them to another practitioner. Keeping them as a client at this point is unprofessional as they will not see the kind of results they want and you will be stressed.

2) Visualization. My son calls it the 'bubble', the protective energy that we wear as we move through the outside world. When I first began to develop my muscle response testing skills and working with energy fields, I was completely over-whelmed. It was like the scene in a sci-fi movie where the alien lands in the middle of New York City and is completely unable to even function in the face of the light and noise all around it. In short, I was a mess. It is extremely difficult to work in that state and the work that you can do is utterly draining. Something had to change. I began visualizing the bubble as a screen, like a screen door. We have these in place so that we can enjoy a breeze and the scent of spring rain wafting through the house, but it keeps out the bugs. Same deal; energy flows in, energy flows out, things that might bite me stay outside where they belong.

3) If you need a little outside help, especially for the people who you know are harder for you to manage your own energy around, you can find it through the alchemy of aromatherapy, flower essences and crystals.

A few examples:

Frankincense oil is considered a protector and clears negative energies. Massaging a drop or two into your hands and feet before you begin working can help diffuse anything stressful as well as help you feel more grounded. Sage oil can do this too – you have probably heard of 'smudging' the burning of sage leaves and stems to cleanse a space. The oil can work in a similar, but much more subtle way, making it more appropriate for an office space.

The Bach Flower Essence 'Walnut' is used for 'oversensitivity to outside influ-ences'. Two drops from a stock bottle can be added to your water bottle in your office and sipped at throughout the day.

Using crystals is slightly higher on the 'woo' spectrum so it won't feel as comforta-ble for some people. Without going into a description of crystal healing and if/why/how it works, we do know that it is true that crystals are sensitive to energetic charge, can hold a charge and emit a specific frequency, which is why they can be used in electronic devices. Therefore, it makes sense that some of these natural frequencies might be helpful in powering up the body's own defense shields. I consulted a guru in the field; Robert Frost, to see what his top suggestions were: 1. Put a quartz crystal in the four corners on your treatment room aiming outwards. (Program them to disperse energies from the room). 2. Black tourmaline is an excellent energy protector. It also uniquely protects others from your energies, too!

It might sound like I am suggesting that you move away from empathy in order to do the work well. This is not the case at all. I used to tell people that I could do this work because I was not empathetic, but that wasn't exactly true. That was me trying imperfectly to find the words to describe the systems I had put into place to keep myself from becoming bogged down, as you see above. The truth is that we absolutely need empathy. It is required. It is what allows us to look at the person on the table and understand what they might be going through and why they have made the decisions they have made. To look at them without judgement knowing that they have done their best. To make sure that they feel heard and loved every minute they are on the table (and yeah, it might be tough-love sometimes, but it is love nonetheless).

Without a certain amount of empathy, it becomes impossible to truly market anything effectively as you cannot clearly imagine what the people that you want to reach are feeling and need. There are a couple of different types of empathy though and the distinction can be important. The first is affective empathy, which means to feel someone else's emotions. Occasionally in our work, we might find that this even extends to literally feeling someone's pain or the symptoms of their disorders as we work with them. This is the type of empathy that it is easy to become overwhelmed by. While it is useful to tap into this in order to understand someone's emotional state and depth of feeling, this is where we need to be sure that we don't become carried away, rendering us useless as practitioners.

The second type is cognitive empathy which has more to do with understanding the desires/wants/needs/intentions and beliefs of another person. There is a word that I learned when working with Seth Godin's altMBA program; the word is 'sonder'. Sonder is defined as the realization that every other person has the same rich inner life that you do. Why is this so hard? We know the way we think about things, that we agonize over decisions, that we weigh our options, that we are narrating our experience to ourselves constantly throughout the day, and yet, it is easy to forget that so is everybody else! Therefore, whatever decision it is that they make, whatever belief it is that they have, you need to understand that it is the sum total of their thoughts and experiences just as yours are. When they say something that is in exact, diametric opposition to everything that you believe, and you think, 'how could anybody be so stupid?' you have to remember that this, whatever it is, is the logical conclusion based on the information that they have at this moment in time. Which isn't to say that we shouldn't do our best to offer them new information to make better choices from, just that we want to be open to wherever they are at right now.

Part of the reason why this is important is because you will be faced with clients that have belief systems very different from your own. If you are working with muscle testing (and somewhat in other modalities), you may find yourself pulling up stress that does not necessarily fit with your understanding of how the world works. I have worked with clients who believe they have been cursed by witches, probed by aliens, and blessed by fairies (not all the same person, thank goodness!). I have also worked with clients who need to have everything proven in triplicate, can barely get their heads around the idea of meridian flow, and would be extremely uncomfortable with any correction using the word 'energetic'. All are fine, all are welcome, all have their reasons for believing as they do. What is important to understand is that the stress that comes up in the session has to do with the individual; it is our job to help them remove that stress and recreate balance. If I have tools in my belt that would make someone uncomfortable, I simply trust that those are not going to come up as the priority correction for that individual. Their body will not ask for something that isn't right for them. So I need to make sure that I am continually muscle testing, using the body's biofeedback to check in, rather than assuming that I know what is best for the person in front of me. Another suggestion is that, rather than always interpreting the information received from muscle testing (or any other kind of analytic tool) ourselves, we can reflect it back to them with questions like, "what does this mean to you?" A question like this allows them to put the information into their own frame, seen through their own lens. It also empowers the individual, making them a part of what is happening in session, rather than just leaving them agog at your 'magical healing powers'. Because, in the end, it's not about you.

Action Plan:

1) Write out a short explanation of what you do and how it works that does not involve you at all. For example; rather than saying "I can reduce pain and help you relax with Reflexology", you might say "Reflexology redirects the energy in your body so you experience less pain and feel more relaxed." Attention is shifted from you and what you do for the client to the modality and how the individual will use it to heal themselves. It's a small difference, but it changes the dynamic.

   _____
   _____
   _____
   _____
   _____
   _____
   _____
   _____
   _____

2) Come up with a ritual for yourself that allows you to not worry about taking on energy. Nothing complex or elaborate; something simple, like shaking your hands and imagining anything negative dispersing, or washing your hands and rinsing it off, or saying a few words quietly to yourself before the session. What the ritual is doesn't really matter, as long as it works for you.

My new ritual:

_____
_____
_____
_____

3) Read good books. I'm a big book geek, so I'm particularly fond of this one! There was a study that showed that reading literary fiction helped improve scores on empathy tests (cited in Appendix 2 at the back). This makes sense; stories that take us out of our usual lives and force us to look at things from another point of view, especially one that is very different than our own, would help us to develop cognitive empathy. You can choose stories with very different protagonists, set in different parts of the world and begin to train your mind to be more elastic, to ask "why did she do that?" rather than judging the action.

"I am balanced and protected."

"I have nothing to give or receive but love."

RULE THREE: IT'S NOT ABOUT YOU

My new ritual

Breathe
Visualize
Balance
Repeat as needed

RULE # 4: IT'S ALL ABOUT RELATIONSHIPS

The first time Ella (name has been changed) came into my office she didn't speak a word to me. Not. One. Word. At 13 years old, she was cutting and had recently been hospitalized for her extreme depression and suicidal talk. Her mother had heard about me and the work I do from a mutual friend and, grasping at straws and thinking that, it couldn't hurt, she brought her daughter in. I explained what I do and how I work to the girl who stared at me impassively. She was compliant but didn't speak or offer anything. As stressors came up for her, and I explained what I was picking up in terms of mental and emotional stress, I would ask "Does this make sense to you?" Each time, she nodded yes. At the end of the session, I figured I would never see her again, even though her mother made a follow up appointment. A few days later I heard from the family – the girl had talked about the session, about me, about how she was feeling all the way home. She was blown away by what muscle testing had revealed about how she was feeling. She was not just willing, but actually happy to come and see me again. What made such an impact on her, this girl who was so fed up with doctors and 'shrinks'? After all, I know the work is amazing, but that it has very little to do with me personally (see previous chapter). I asked her years later and her answer was basically that, in not trying to force her to talk, as the rest of them had, she felt completely understood. If I had tried to make her talk to me, she would have given me the answers she thought I wanted to hear, but we never would have gotten anywhere.

In all businesses today, personal relationships are important. But in fields that depend on a client feeling understood and helped they are not just important but essential. Without good relationships, you have no business at all.

Does this seem obvious? Probably, especially if you have been in some kind of customer-service oriented job before. But this kind of work, because of the intimacy of it, tests the way you work with and connect to people in a way that most other careers simply don't. I have sat in the hospital with a client in labour keeping her as grounded as possible so she could make the decisions needed about what was best for herself and her baby. I have done house calls late at night. I have taken midnight phone calls, worked late at night/ early in the morning/on a Sunday/Holidays, whatever. People will tell you that it is essential to have boundaries in this field, and it's true that you do. But what's even more true is that you will grow to love these people and to care deeply what happens to them and they will ask you to be there in moments that matter most to them as a result. The important thing to remember is that you always have choices about this – who you are willing to 'break the rules' for and what rules you are not willing to compromise on.

While most people understand the need for kindness and understanding with their clients, this sometimes can fall by the wayside once we move from the practitioner-client relationship to the practitioner-practitioner or instructor-student ones. While I work with several modalities of alternative health, muscle testing and energy-work (called Kinesiology in some countries) is absolutely my specialty. While it is amazing for working with almost any problem you can think of, it is much less known than a system like Reiki or herbalism. As a result, once you move into the ranks of professionals, it is a ridiculously small world where everyone knows everyone, at least by reputation if not in person.

This is why I find it absolutely mind-boggling when people don't play nice. I attended a conference a couple years ago where I was one of the presenters. It was a small conference, with under a hundred attendees, so as you can imagine most people are aware of what other people are doing all of the time. So here's the question: if you are stranded in a small hotel with a hundred people who you will be spending the next four days with, morning 'til night, and you know that you will be seeing these people again next year at this event and until you either retire from the field or die because this is a tiny little community of people passionate enough to keep coming back to these events – if all this was true, do you think you could manage to be polite and friendly? For four days? And yet it is shocking how many don't! In a field where we preach empathy, the need to forgive and universal love, do you think we could ignore small perceived slights? In a group that claims to want to spread the word of what we do throughout the world, could we make more room for new practitioners and in-structors, rather than feeling like there will be less pie for us now? I feel like I should add a caveat to this, which is that I personally have felt welcomed and loved most of the time when at conferences and events. But I understand that this is not everyone's experience; this is coming partly from observing others and hearing the complaints of other practitioners and students.

> In a field where we preach empathy, the need to forgive and universal love, do you think we could ignore small perceived slights?

In his book *Leaders Eat Last*, Simon Sinek argues that our biology evolved for us to need a tribe that allows us to feel safe. That in order for us to survive as humans thousands of years ago, we had to feel like we could fully trust our group. Our neurotransmitters developed as ways to reward and incentivize us for behaviours that would benefit the group. This is one of the reasons why we feel better when we give to charity or do something nice for someone we know – we get little hits of oxytocin that reward us for these behaviours. When we try to behave in a cutthroat "it's only business" way, it might seem like we are benefitting ourselves, but it goes against our primal nature to belong to and take care of our tribe. When a business deliberately encourages a culture of competition for approval and resources it sets the entire company back in the long term. We move ahead exponentially when we feel safe and taken care of, not just as an industry, but as individuals. It is better for your bottom line to help and support your fellow practitioners than it is for you to be in stiff competition.

We all know people who do this naturally, those who freely give their time and knowledge and make new people feel welcome. We naturally gravitate towards those people. I have been so blessed in my field to, for some reason that I do not fully understand, have been taken in by some of the Greats who will patiently answer my questions and listen to me, even when I am repeatedly a pain in the ass.

The business world can sometimes be portrayed as competitive – after all, for me to make the sale, it means you didn't, right? But the holistic health field has the potential to be much more friendly and inclusive if we let it. Really if you look at it, we have a nearly infinite market at our disposal because there isn't anyone who couldn't benefit from improved physical, mental or emotional health. Most adults are walking piles of compensation patterns devised to get us through the day without falling over. What I'm saying is, there is plenty of dysfunction to go around, so there really isn't any reason for us to compete for it. Especially once you take into account the fact that no two practitioners are exactly alike. Even if we have experienced the same training, we both bring our own experience and energy to the table, so people will respond to it differently.

A side thought to this is the need to show respect across modalities. Of course you think your chosen one is the best, that's why you chose it! But surely you can see situations and individuals who could benefit from another type of treatment? I used to make a point of getting to know the other practitioners in my area (I have slowed down with this recently because, here in the middle-of-nowhere, there is a serious lack of other practitioners, but even so I am creating a network). If I had a client come in telling me that they absolutely love their chiropractor, or that they were really impressed with a new naturopath or that they just had an acupuncture session that changed their life, I always asked who they saw. And if I heard the same name more than once, I would make contact. I would simply call them up or send an email, mention that we seem to have some clients in common and that I had heard good things about them and ask if they would like to meet. After that we might arrange a meeting, I would tour through their facility if possible and we would probably exchange cards and I would ask for a special discount for my clients. Then I have someone who I have met personally and have contact info for when my client needs it. So when I have someone on my table who I feel would benefit from seeing s chiropractor for example, something I am nowhere near qualified to do, I can say "here's a card; I met her myself and she seems great and we have clients in common that speak very highly of her. If you mention that I referred you, you'll get a $10 discount." This is impressive for your client because they know that you truly are looking out for their best interests – you are not just trying to keep them coming back to you but want them to do whatever they need to in order to feel their best. At the same time, it raises your profile with the other practitioners; ideally they will return the favour and if they have someone in their office looking for a good BodyTalk/ aromatherapy/Raynor massage, etc. person, they will send them in to see you. Building your network in this way adds value to your client, raises your profile in your community and will probably introduce you to some fascinating people in the process.

> It is about solving problems for someone else – showing them an option that is going to change their life for the better.

I remember my very first trade show that I worked as a holistic health entrepreneur. I was 22 years-old. I had my business cards that I had printed myself on special perforated business card stock from Wal-Mart and brochures filled with Papyrus font (as all true holistic health professionals do before they know better). My business name was Nurture by Nature and I was ready to rock the tiny town I lived in. All these years later, I honestly can't remember if I got a single client directly out of that weekend. Here's what I do remember - reconnecting with a friend that I hadn't seen in a few months who then introduced me to the guy running the booth three down from me. That guy became one of my very best friends. Fast-forward to the present and I have worked on him, his wife and kids and he is a great cheerleader for my work. If I had ignored him in order to 'work my booth', I would have missed out on so much. At Networking events and trade shows, where people are counting how many business cards they were able to hand out in the evening as if there is a prize for quantity, I am much more in favour of making one or two real connections. Those people that you really click with and get a chance to speak with in depth, those are the ones who will advocate for you and what you do. Even if they never become your clients themselves, when they hear someone complain about their stiff neck or recent diagnosis, they are going to think of you and pass your name on. It's not about how many fans you have, it's about how passionate your fans are. 1000 people following you on Facebook is of less benefit to you than 10 people who are so excited about your events that they share them and talk about them to others.

Which of course leads into the topic of social media which is a little bit controversial here. Because we need to use this for marketing, but relationships that exist solely online are not the same as those where we connect face-to-face. The lack of real eye contact, the inability to read body language properly, to be in the other person's energy field, means that it is difficult if not impossible to really get to know anyone and build up any level of trust. Ideally, social media can be used to maintain the relationship at a distance – to allow you to remain connected, after making the initial contact and give you a way of touching base as you go. While it has become the norm to complain about social media and its' downsides and the amount of time it can absorb, I am incredibly grateful for the tribe of practitioners around the world it allows me to connect with daily. Every single day, I get a chance to speak with people as passionate as I am about our weird little industry from all over the place. How amazing that this is possible! Because of this, we can attend a yearly conference and meet amazing people and keep up with them throughout the year so we still feel connected when we see them again. Social media allows us to see what others in our field are struggling with and help them out when possible and it lets us see when our clients need us so we can offer support. There are ways for us to use this for maximum effect and we will continue to discuss this throughout the workbook.

Action Plan:

1) Find your tribe. Is there an association for your modalities in your area? A chapter of Holistic Chamber of Commerce? Something similar? Find a group of people who work in the same industry and therefore have some of the same challenges and joys that you do. Go to a meeting or two and see if you want to join.

2) Find at least three people or businesses in your area who have complementary skill sets to yours and make contact. Remember to make it about them, not about you. "I'm looking for a naturopath I can refer people to when they need testing," or "I sometimes suggest nutritional products for my clients and want to have a great place in mind where they can get them." Health food stores and gyms are great places to check out on top of looking for other practitioners.

Ideas about who to contact:

_____
_____
_____
_____

3) Make yourself available to others in your field. You may not feel comfortable with something as official as becoming a mentor at this point in time, but you can do basic things like join Facebook groups for practitioners and participate in a thoughtful way when people ask questions. Your experience in this area might be exactly what someone is looking for to help them get past a specific hurdle that has been keeping them back.

"I attract the clients and colleagues that are right for me."

"I support and nurture my tribe."

RULE FOUR: IT'S ALL ABOUT RELATIONSHIPS

RULE # 5: 'MARKETING' IS NOT A DIRTY WORD

This harks back to the original thought of working it like a business – some people have real issues with the idea of 'marketing' what we do. At one International conference I was preparing a presentation for, when I pitched my idea to speak about marketing and personal branding, I was told that the idea of marketing as Specialized Kinesiology practitioners leaves "a sulfurous smell". I have spoken about marketing and personal branding at several SK conferences now and, it's true, some people are visibly uncomfortable with the idea. There's that image of the slimy salesman that comes to mind for so many people. Insincere, only out for himself, this is the opposite of how most practitioners in the holistic health field see themselves, so it can be hard to balance this image with the need to promote what we do. When you think of the word 'marketing' you may have an idea of television commercials, tacky billboards, or an irritating jingle that you can't get out of your head, but this isn't the approach that we are going for. Marketing can mean putting quality content out into the world that helps people who are aligned with our energy and goals find us. It's that simple.

Marketing means making information readily available in an attractive way. It is about solving problems for someone else – showing them an option that is going to change their life for the better. This is totally different than the way most people think of marketing, which basically equates to shouting in someone's face about what you want to sell them. This is missing the point. Seth Godin would say that marketing is a chance to serve, and if you look at it in this way, as an act of generosity and help, then it changes what you do and how you do it.

Any time you put out content that explains what you do and who you are in a way that might inspire people to work with you, that's marketing. Yes, ads in print and online journals, radio, etc. but it's more than that. Every post on Facebook, every blog post, every open house, every time one of your clients tells a friend about you – this is marketing, and these things are free! The question becomes: are you leveraging them properly?

Think about that greasy salesman again. Have you ever been to a 'Networking event'? I'm kind of introverted, so these are Hell as far as I'm concerned. A crowd of people who often are just counting how many hands they can get their business cards into. There are some people who do these events well, but many fall into the Salesman category – they are there to talk about what they sell and why you want to buy it and very little thought or attention is given to who you are and what you need. If you buy into the premise of the last section though and are paying attention to the relationships themselves and not just what you think that they can do for you, that it's not really about you; then you won't be That Guy.

Because you are listening to what people are actually saying and hearing what they need, then figuring out how what you do can help them, you are putting their needs ahead of your own. Then, because it's not about you, you can discuss the advantages and benefits of your chosen modality. You can talk about it separate from yourself; not that you are a miracle worker, but from the belief that the human body is amazing and can heal itself if given the tools and opportunity to do so. This is the real reason that I have so much trouble with Networking events. I can stand up in from of a room of a thousand people and talk about Specialized Kinesiology without breaking a sweat. I believe 100% in my work and truly believe that if it isn't the most amazing thing you've ever heard of, you probably don't understand it. But attend an event where we go around the room with the generic instructions to give your name, your business and "tell us a little about yourself"? Terror. And while I can give a keynote about muscle testing and fill 90 minutes happily, at the Networking event I will probably say something short and lame in order to be allowed to sit down quietly again.

Before you can begin a real conversation about marketing, you need to have a clear idea in your head of who you want to work with. Ideally you have already begun working with the Business Plan in the back of this book, using the information from the first section and have given this some thought. In the event that you haven't though, let's take a moment here to talk about the ideal client, also sometimes called the 'avatar'.

An avatar is described as a representative of a group of people. The avatar is the perfect user of your system; the one that all the information is for. When thinking about your marketing strategy, you want to spend some time designing this avatar. Who are they? Gender? Age? Education level? Income? (See the Action Plan at the end of this chapter for more ideas). When we understand thoroughly who it is that we want to connect with, we do a better job of tailoring our message so that it can appeal to that individual. We can see what problems they might have that our work can solve. And, remembering again that it is all about relationships, you want to describe the kind of person that you really and truly want to work with. Think about that image of the salesman again – the one who sees everyone around him as a 'mark' or a 'sucker' or something of that sort. If this is the way that we are visualizing our clients, then there is nothing to build on.

The more clearly you can see this ideal client in your head, the easier it is to navigate the information that we are constantly being bombarded with about marketing; you can already picture how they spend their time and what would be appealing. This will influence your marketing; not just your colour scheme and word choice, but also where you choose to spend your advertising dollars as you think about the places where your avatar will be consuming the content. There is a worksheet included in the Action Plan to help you create this persona. Start with one (the most important one obviously, the client nearest to your heart that you most want to work with) but if you have various niches that your work extends into, you can create a new avatar for each of these. Just remember that it is far more powerful to focus on delivering an amazing experience to one group of people than it is to try to please everyone.

Now unless the avatar that you have created is a mountain-top-dwelling hermit-luddite , chances are they are online. Which means that the internet, in one aspect or another is going to play a role in your marketing plan because this is probably where your avatar is spending a good portion of their time. I recently read that we don't call it 'online marketing' anymore, we just call it 'marketing'. The 'online' part is inevitable. Are you leveraging social media in a way that makes sense for your business model? Remember earlier when we discussed how it's all about relationships? It turns out that one of the things that your clients want more of is you. That's kind of sweet don't you think? When you post pictures of your kids, your cats, your vacation; when you share the bits of you that are not directly related to work but which make you who you are, this helps turn you into a person and not just a business in the eyes of your clients. You are more relatable and can be perceived as more genuine.

Now, a few years ago all of the books advocating social media marketing talked extensively about setting boundaries and the importance of separating personal and business accounts and all of that. But here's the thing; there is no such thing as online privacy anymore. If you think that you can post pictures of yourself partying on your Facebook page and your clients aren't going to notice because you have separate accounts for business, then you've got another thing coming. Assume that everything you post anywhere online can and will be seen by everyone. Your mother, your clients, your employees/bosses. Understanding that then, make sure that what you post is congruent with the image you are trying to maintain. I have an acquaintance from high school who is a DJ/musician in a big city. His social media is filled with pictures of himself with his tongue sticking out alongside scantily clad models, obviously drinking heavily. This is congruent with the image he is marketing with – he wants to be perceived as a rock-god who knows where the party is happening. This look doesn't work so well for a yoga instructor. As we will go over in a later chapter, we need to be authentic with our message and people are pretty good at spotting hypocrisy.

When I was running an office with other practitioners, I had separate accounts on various social media platforms for the business. And yes, I would post fun personal pictures as well (because as you may have gathered by now, that's the kind of place it was), but it was still very different from the way I speak when I'm representing myself and not the group. I realized that in some ways, it's much easier to market for a business. "We have a sale coming up!" "We have a special event next weekend!" "We have a few openings still on Friday if anyone is interested!" This is easier than saying "I'm running a class, I have an opening, I sell this product". It's hard to do without feeling aggressive or like you are imposing on people's time and attention. (Aside: I am well aware of how Ultra-Canadian the last sentence might sound as I apologize for taking up any of someone's attention.

Perhaps this isn't an issue for you. Sorry.) Some people try to get around this by being kind of sneaky with their attempts at marketing. I don't think that works either; there is an assumption inherent in that which says that you think you're smarter than the people reading it and that they won't notice what you're doing. Personally, I don't think there's anything wrong with making an 'ask' every once in a while_ and making it very clear that is what you are doing. If you are the kind of person who is generous with their time and knowledge, people are often happy to comply when you ask directly for something. What does that look like? How about something really clear like; "I have this new product I am selling. I am excited about it because I think it will help people with ___. I would really appreciate it if a few of my friends were willing to try it out and let me know what they think." It's direct, but it's still a soft sell. The ball is in their court.

You have probably heard the term 'content marketing'. Content is King is how the saying goes. We live in an information age and people are constantly, daily using the internet as a way of learning something that they need right now. Content Marketing Institute, an online resource for all things related to content marketing (so yes, they may have a vested interest in this) defines it as such, "Content marketing is a marketing technique of creating and distributing valuable, relevant and consistent content to attract and acquire a clearly defined audience – with the objective of driving profitable customer action." The key word here is valuable – the value of the information is what causes people to seek out this information rather than tune it out or avoid it like they might for other forms of advertising. If you can provide the information that they are looking for and do it consistently (double bonus points if you can do it with style or a measure of humour) then these people become your clients. Think about how you feel when it comes time to make a big-ticket purchase; do you feel more comfortable choosing a brand that you have heard of, read about and trust? When you are creating good content, you establish a level of rapport and trust with your potential clients before you even meet.

How do you come up with content? Try this: make a list of the questions you hear the most about your chosen modality. A few examples: How does it work? What happens in a session? Can it help __?. If you can come up with a few questions that you can answer, then you can post these answers somewhere, in some form, which people will then find.

Questions I get the most often about my work/modality:

_____
_____
_____
_____
_____
_____
_____
_____

Here are a few examples of ways you can begin getting valuable content out into the world and being of service to your clients:

Website. You do have a website, right? This is an easy way for you to get content out: simply write a little information about your modality, answer some of the frequently asked questions you get or offer some useful resources. If you want to try blogging, that can be a fun way of creating content for the website that encourages people to interact with you by commenting or asking questions. A website doesn't have to be complicated, flashy or expensive. It should however look clean and modern and be full of your own material – don't use pictures or information owned by others that could create a copyright issue for you in the future.

Infographics: if you're not comfortable with your writing skills, infographics might be a fun way for you to get your ideas out since they are much more visual. Infographics tend to do really well on Pinterest.

Podcasts: Recording yourself speaking about a topic and allowing people to stream from your website or a service or set up as a downloadable file.

Videos: This can range from professional videos to more casual vlogs and can be posted either on your website or on a YouTube or Vimeo channel.

Which of these is best? Well that really depends upon you. Personally, I feel like the more ways that you can get your message out the better, since not everyone has the same learning style and will respond differently to different types of messages. Some of us are readers and will immediately want long-form content to dive into when researching something new. Some aren't but would happily listen to a podcast while driving to work every morning. The other advice is to stick with your strengths. I love the way that the internet has leveled the playing field in so many ways and given people access to information in new ways, but one of the irritating things about that is the abundance of extremely poorly written content that you must wade through sometimes in order to find anything that is relevant. Be honest with yourself about your strengths and weakness as a communicator. I have a friend who is a ridiculously good salesman; put him in front of a crowd and five minutes later they'll all be waving their credit cards in the air and half in love. But when I have to read anything he has written I want to tear out my own eyes in order to make the pain stop. He should stick to videos, where his natural charisma will shine through and override his inability to spell or use proper grammar. We all have our weak spots.

Once you have created interesting content, your social media accounts become the channels of distribution. If your stuff is valuable; informative, funny, thoughtful, whatever; all you need are a few good fans and it will spread from there.

There is a cheat for this too. It is always best to create your own content, but the abundance of information available online means that, if you absolutely cannot make yourself create new things, you can take on the role of a curator and put together other people's stuff. For example, Pinterest boards are basically curated content – people have found images and articles from all over the web and put them together under a heading like 'Gluten Free Nom Noms' or 'Party Ideas for Birthday Cats'. You can follow these boards and click through all of the information there, saving what might be relevant to your life on your own boards. This happens in blog form when people post articles listing the 'Top Ten Best

Websites for _____'. Not a bad way to get your feet wet as well as building rapport with others in your field. In order for this to work well you will need to seek out great content on a regular basis (consider this when reading Rule Nine later).

Remember that while people will tell you that they don't like advertising, what they actually don't like is the interruption. The commercial that makes them wait three minutes before they get back to their show, the glaring billboard that breaks up the beautiful scenery. When the advertising is imparting something of value no one minds it. No one complains about clothing designers having full page ads in fashion magazines, because the ad is offering an idea of fashion and beauty that is appreciated by the kind of people who would be buying that magazine. People deliberately search for and watch certain commercials on YouTube every day because they are funny, they then share them with all of their friends on social media. Obviously, this is our end goal – to create the kind of advertising that doesn't interrupt; that people will actively seek out rather than avoid because it is interesting and informative and helps to create rapport.

Action Plan:

1) Create some content with solid information behind it that could be useful to the kind of people you want to work with, and then give it away. Don't try to use this first bit to convince people to book appointments or buy a product, just create something useful and put it out into the world. Create trust and relationships.

2) Make an ask (not connected with the above content which you are giving away, no strings attached). This doesn't even have to be in connection with your business because at this point it's not really about using this to find more clients/students/customers, it's about stretching your comfort zone a little bit. Most people are uncomfortable just coming out and asking for something that is important to them, but I think you will be surprised how happy people are to be able to give you something worthwhile. Some things you might consider asking your group of acquaintances for: an introduction to someone influential, a referral, to check your newly created content and offer feedback, a ride, help with a difficult task. Ask and you shall receive. See what happens. And remember to be generous in return when the time is right. Karma, Law of Attraction, Golden Rule, etc...

What can you ask for?

_____
_____
_____
_____

3) Create your avatar. Begin by describing this person in as much detail as you can. Think about the things we discussed before: age, gender, income and education

level, but also some slightly deeper questions. To me, the most important questions are more about how this person spends their time. Where do they hang out? What do they enjoy doing? These are the questions that let you see what you have in common with this person, thereby giving you some common ground that you can use to build your relationship and reach out to them. Use the worksheet on the next page to do this properly.

4) Assess your strengths and weaknesses when it comes to communication. Do you get your ideas across most clearly when speaking? When writing? When drawing a picture or through interpretive dance (no judgement)? Figure out your top form of communication and then focus on that one first. Find someone you admire who excels at that type of content and watch/listen to/read some of their material making notes of what aspects of it you enjoy most.

My strongest communication method: _____

My weakest link:_____

My super-awesome role-model for this:_____

Avatar Creation Worksheet

What is an Avatar? Basically, what you are doing here is helping yourself define very clearly the ideal client – the person that you want to reach out to and work with. Spending a little time on this allows you to be precise in the way that you are marketing and spend your time and money in the best way possible. Does this feel silly for some people? Maybe a little. After all, in some ways this is basically the adult equivalent of creating an imaginary friend. A couple things that it might be helpful to remember:

There are no wrong answers. This is about who you want to work with, so don't worry if it sounds a little odd when you write it all out. We're not trying to please everyone – maybe the oddballs are your ideal clients and that is totally ok. In fact, when putting this together you actually may want to focus on some of the ways that your avatar is different from the people around them. Knowing how they are quirky and what sets them apart from the crowd is what allows you to connect with them on a deeper level.

This can be fluid and can change. You are not stuck with this indefinitely. You can add things, and take them away as you grow. You can add more avatars in the future to represent the various aspects of your business. You, my friend, have options, so don't be afraid to jump in and have fun with this. If you know that your business has many different avenues, you may wish to photocopy this before you begin so that you can use it for more Avatars later. Or you can go to www.gemskinesiology.com and download it again,

The basics:

The first few blanks are designed to give you an overview so you can visualize the individual. It doesn't have to be too complicated (there is no need to describe the exact shade of hazel her eyes are, unless you're into that sort of thing).

Gender:_____

Age:_____

Marital status:_____

Children:_____

Income:_____

Education:_____

Employment role:_____

To make this whole process easier for yourself, give your avatar a name:

Goals (what are their big dreams, their big Why?)

_____
_____
_____
_____
_____
_____

Objectives (how are they going to achieve those goals?):

_____
_____
_____
_____
_____
_____

Values (if they were going to choose their Core Values from the list at the back like you did, what would they be? Are they the same as yours, or different?):

_____
_____
_____
_____
_____

Pain points / problems that need solving:

_____
_____
_____
_____

Current sources of information: Books, magazines, websites, conferences, gurus, etc.

_____
_____
_____
_____

Where do they spend their time? What are they doing when they aren't at work?

_____
_____
_____
_____

What about your work/products/services would appeal to them?

_____
_____
_____
_____

What are their possible objections to obtaining your products/services ?

_____
_____
_____
_____

"I am comfortable sharing my work
with the world."

"I offer valuable information
to all."

RULE FIVE: MARKETING IS
NOT A DIRTY WORD

Draw your Avatar here

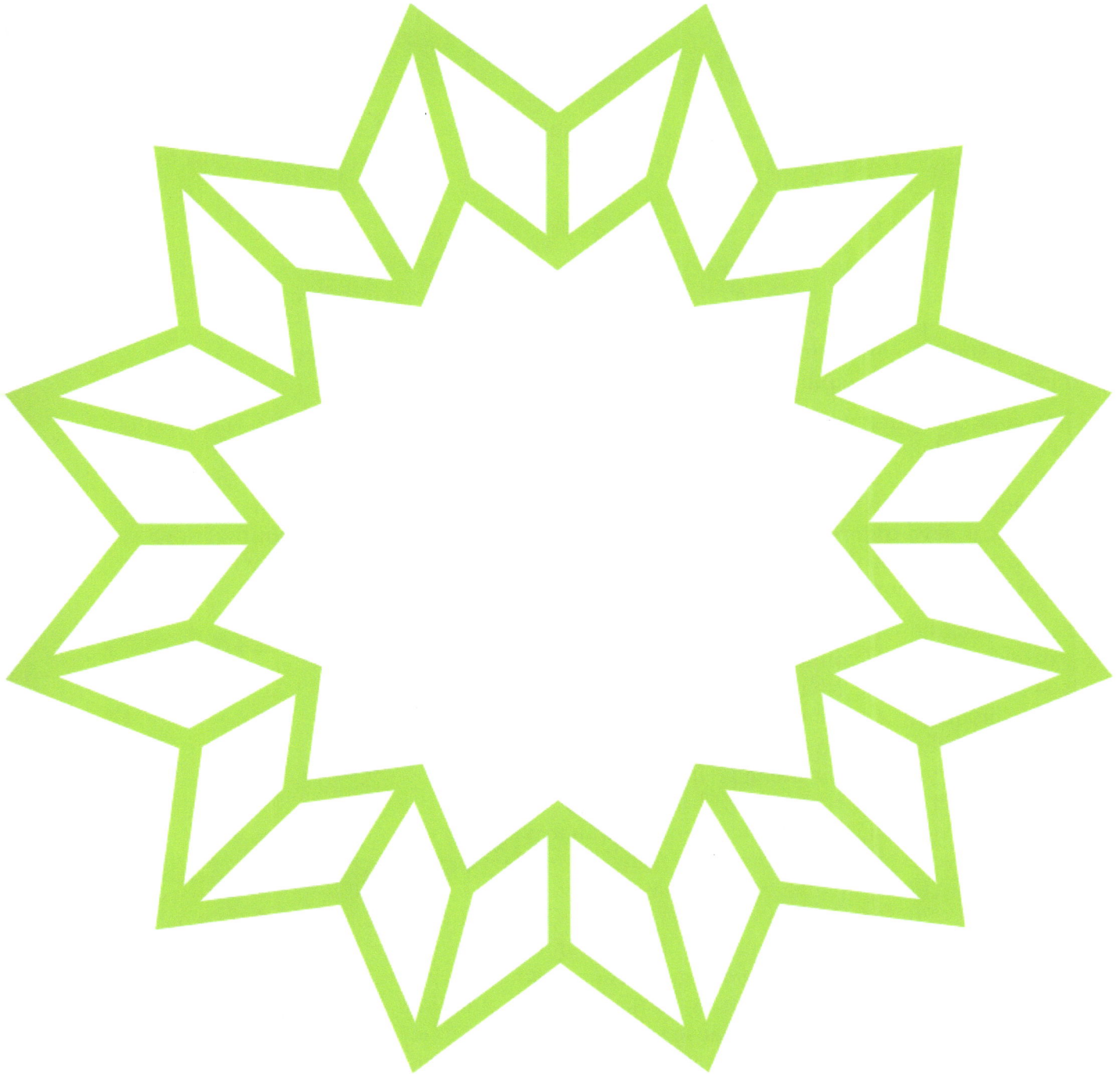

RULE # 6: FIND YOUR SOAPBOX

What is the issue in the world that makes you insane? The problem you know you could solve with the creative use of your holistic therapist skills? The story you know how to tell that will leave the room breathless?

This is your soapbox.

In the late 1800's people would use a soapbox (or another crate that goods had been shipped in) as a little stage when they wanted to make a speech or express their political opinions in a public space. Somebody getting up on a soapbox would draw a crowd and provide some entertainment. The same thing happens today, even though for most of us, our soapbox is more on the metaphorical side.

Find something that you can stand on top of, something bigger than yourself. This doesn't have to be a huge or complex issue, it could be something simple. But find something you would be willing to stand up for; something that makes your eyes shine and reminds you why you care about what we do in the first place. You are allowed to have more than one soapbox; I have different ones that I get up on when I am speaking within my industry than when I am speaking with the general public. People who know me well will probably ask at this point when am I *not* on a soapbox, but it does happen on occasion.

This is also known as finding your 'why?', as in the greater reason why you do what you do. Your why is separate from the what and the how and is the most important message to understand and to convey clearly. For an entire book detailing the reasons why your why is the most important, check out Simon Sinek's book "Start with Why", or view his TED Talk on YouTube. (I am pretty sure that is the most I've ever written the word 'why' in one sentence that didn't involve the dialogue of a 3-year -old). Most of the time when we speak with people about our jobs, we tell them what we do, occasionally sprinkling in a bit of the 'how', but rarely do we tell them 'why'. Your why is important because it reveals your motivation, your spirit, your soapbox. It is bigger than you and for that reason is inspiring to the people around you. Even if you say that the reason why you go to work is because you need to make money, that trail can be followed to reveal your deeper purpose. True, no one is going to be inspired to work with you by you saying that you want to make more money, so my follow up question to you would be (wait for it), why? Why do you want to make more money? What would that mean for

WHY?

you? Chances are if you have ended up in the holistic health field, you have a why that has to do with being able to serve others, to help them feel well, to solve problems that you see around you. Make sure that when you are speaking with people about who you are and what you do, you include these reasons and not just a list of your credentials. Seeing a list of the courses that you have taken does not inspire anyone; reading your diatribe about working with kids diagnosed with learning difficulties might. Once people understand why you are in this field, you can then explain to them how you work and what exactly you do; the point is to start with this oft-neglected piece and work out from there.

I think that we are afraid to do this sometimes because it seems too vulnerable. It's something that maybe gets drummed into us as teens and young adults; that it's not cool to care too much about anything, or that if you show your hand and reveal what it is that you really want, someone will take it away from you. It's true, this happens. There are people who will think that knowing something intimate about you gives them an advantage or something that they can use against you in the future. But for every person like that, I believe there are many more who will look at it and be inspired and you can't reach them without reaching the others too! The truth of the matter is, thanks to authors/speakers like Brene Brown championing the power of vulnerability in recent years, more and more people are beginning to respect and admire those willing to be vulnerable. Because of the transparency inherent in our social media saturated lives, we are not expected to be shiny and happy all of the time any more in order to be successful. You are allowed to show the bits that aren't perfect, to reveal your motivations and to show that there are steps that have to be taken in order to get from here to there. I think this is a step in the right direction.

Chances are, if you were to take a minute right now and think about the people and companies that you find the most inspiring, they would have in common that they have a clear sense of why they do what they do and they convey that message clearly to the public. For an example of this, think about some of the charities that you have seen fundraising campaigns for. Do you see brochures featuring a new well and some mosquito nets encouraging you to give money for clean drinking water and to keep malaria at bay? No, you see pictures of children. The well and the nets may be how we are going to accomplish something, but the 'why' is about healthy children able to grow up. No-one wants to spend their hard-earned money on mosquito nets for other people, but everyone believes that the children of the world deserve a chance. Sometimes it's just about making sure that you are on the right soapbox.

Once you have identified a cause or two that you want to stand up for, you need to find your medium. We are not all public speakers, we are not all writers, but we can all find some way to express ourselves that feels authentic and allows the message to shine through clearly. While I enjoy public speaking, writing is what I love. I like the degree of intimacy and yet distance that it offers. (That might just be the most 'introvert' statement ever written.) The fact that it is not immediate means that I can say what I mean in the moment, but then look back, review and refine, make sure the words are right. And you may resonate with my informal style of writing, or you may find it annoying, but unlike when I stand up and talk in front of a room of people, what is on the page is there in black and white, not subject to memory.

Last summer I was teaching an advanced Specialized Kinesiology class to a new group in the US. I mentioned that a certain symbol was pagan in origin and moved on with the point of the lesson. At the lunch break, one of the women in the class mentioned that she had some confusion about one of the points we had been discussing and admitted that she had switched off a little because of her shock that I was showing them satanic symbols. I assured her that there is nothing of the sort in the class and was struggling to understand what she was talking about. The others listening were baffled – they agreed that the word 'satanic' had never been uttered. In the end we realized it was her own filter – I had said the word 'pagan' and she had heard the other. I was so glad that she had asked me the question so that I had a chance to explain, but if she hadn't, she may have gone home with the completely wrong idea about course content, simply because her own brain had substituted words. That type of thing doesn't happen with books!

How do you feel comfortable expressing yourself? We touched on this a little bit earlier when discussing the need for creating useful content. If you like to write but the idea of sitting down and creating long-form content feels daunting, you could consider short social media posts. Twitter is an amazing way of honing your writing skills because if having a 240-character limit doesn't force you to be concise and clear in your message then nothing will. When we put it into context like that the perennial excuse of "I don't have time" disappears as well. You don't have time to write 240 characters? That's ridiculous, if you have time to scroll through social media (and you know you do it) then you have time to post something worthwhile there.

The Facebook Live feature is great for people who would prefer to speak to an audience rather than write, but without the jitteriness of facing a room full of people. These can be long or short and are free to use, so while it may not be as slick as recording yourself properly and setting up a vlog, it can be a fun way of seeing if video works for you as a medium.

Action Plan:

1) Think about some of the companies or individuals that you feel inspired by and choose to spend your money with. Why do they do what they do? See if you could write a vision statement for their company or brand based on what you know about them. Once you have done this, check out the companies' website – many of them will have a vision or mission statement somewhere for the public to see. See how close yours is to the official version. The companies with the most effective marketing are the ones who are able to convey their 'why' in everything they do.

Favourite company #1 and their vision:

_____

_____

Favourite company #2 and their vision:

_____
_____

(How close were you?)

2) Why are you here? Many of us end up in the holistic health world because we have
had the experience of being disenchanted with the allopathic medical system after
a diagnosis or a negative intervention. Others end up here because they feel a calling, still others because there is someone they love that badly needed help.
Whatever it is, can you find a way to share your story? When you put it out there
for the world to see you offer inspiration, but also a window into your own
motivation. There can be power in wearing your heart on your sleeve. Even if you
don't decide to make this story public, writing it down for yourself and finding
some clarity on it can help you to focus and build your own brand story. On the
following page is a brainstorming sheet for you to write down why you do what
you do. Write down all of the reasons, even the ones that don't feel as lofty or
inspiring. If at first you find yourself with vague answers like 'to help people',
continue asking yourself questions until you become more specific; why do you
want to help people? Who are these people? Why do they need your help? Once
you have a list in front of you, see which ones you resonate with the strongest.
Could any of these become a soapbox that you can stand on in order to get your
message out in a clear and interesting way to the people that you are wanting to
help?

My Story of how I got here:

_____
_____
_____
_____
_____
_____
_____
_____
_____
_____
_____
_____

3) How do you want to get your message out? See if a specific medium lends itself
more strongly to your message than another. For example, if your why involves
working with young mothers in the city you live in, finding a community centre

where you could speak directly to that group makes a lot of sense. If your message (like mine), tends to be for far flung individuals in a tiny niche market scattered all over the world, that's where the beauty of the internet comes in and you are going to want to try your hand at blogging or making videos or anything that felt inspiring to you from the previous chapter on marketing.

The best mediums for my avatar and my Why:

_____
_____
_____

"I know WHY I do what I do."

"My passion and purpose shine through."

RULE SIX: FIND YOUR
SOAPBOX

All the Reasons WHY

The most
important one:

RULE #7: WALK THE TALK

If you're going to get up on a soapbox, you'd better be sure that you are walking the talk. This is where people begin talking about 'authenticity', a word so overused in the marketing and pop-business word currently that it makes me vaguely nauseous just to type it, though I have had to several times while putting this together. There is a reason for the hype; authenticity is maybe the most important thing we can strive for in marketing right now.

There are a few reasons for this. One is that people have become disenchanted with traditional advertising. The gimmicks and manipulations that have been used to sell us things for the past few generations – they are overdone; we see through them. Like the bombastic cry of "But wait; there's more!" so many of these have become clichés of such epic proportions that it is hard to imagine the time when employees were trained to respond to customers in this way. In a world full of noise and artificial connection, one of the things that your clients crave is real communication.

I know full well that I have had clients in the past, who don't really need to be coming in as often as they do. They ask when they need to come back, and I suggest a few months from now to check in unless anything comes up that is creating stress in the meantime that they feel like they need to work on. And they immediately book for two weeks in the future. If you do any type of bodywork, you have probably had this experience too. For so many people, a practitioner or therapist of some kind is the only time they experience safe, loving, non-sexual touch. It's the time they feel listened to. They have a real bond with you and are willing to keep coming back because that is a rarity in their world. If we are not authentic with these people, we are betraying the trust they put in us. If they can't trust us, then they cannot possibly have any loyalty, which means that they may be clients for now, but they won't be when they get another offer.

The first time that this truly hit me was ages ago when we were living in a tiny town in Northern Saskatchewan (yeah, I mentioned this before) when I was writing for a local paper. I was grocery shopping one evening with my twins who were almost two at the time and my husband. We pushed the cart through the till and were making polite small talk with the woman behind the till. She said something along the lines of "It's great that we have all these organic products now. It's nice to see someone practicing what they preach." She told me she had been reading my columns and recognized my picture. I had no idea that the woman who ran through our groceries most weekends was reading my columns on Fridays, this was the first time she had mentioned it. But she had been reading and she noticed the kind of food I was buying and had come to the conclusion that I was sincere in what I was telling the world. This was so long ago but it stuck with me; what if I had been nasty or harsh with this person? What if she had looked at my family and I and decided that I was full of it? If you've ever lived in a small town then you know how quickly a reputation can be damaged. I have tried to remember that lesson since. Where I live now, the lesson is even more pronounced as I am the Crazy-White-Lady-With-The-Goats; highly visible in my Costa Rican Tico community!

The second reason has more to do with you and your stress levels. You see, being authentic is easy. Making the transition to being authentic can be hard because it is scary to be vulnerable and all your insecurities might come up to the surface. But once you're there, authenticity is easy to maintain because it simply means being yourself, which is much less energy-intensive than trying to keep up an illusion of perfection (which usually isn't really fooling anyone anyway). Do you believe in the Law of Attraction? Whether you call it that or The Secret or Power of Positive Thinking, or Karma doesn't really matter, what it boils down to is the idea that what you put out into the universe is what is reflected back to you. This is not to say that authenticity requires a veneer of positivity in order to help you to meet your goals, nor is it an excuse to let you off the hook when you don't feel like doing something. Rather, this information is here is to underline the idea that you - the real true you in all your messy glory - have a vibrational frequency all your own. And some people are going to be attracted to that and you will amplify each other to new and wondrous heights, and some

> This is not to say that authenticity requires a veneer of positivity in order to help you to meet your goals, nor is it an excuse to let you off the hook when you don't feel like doing something.

people will be repelled by it and it's really for the best if you stay out of each other's way. When you just are who you are, this frequency is clear and easy to read and there is no confusion or ambiguity for people. It's a time saver for both of you really.

I have spoken about this idea of attracting exactly the right clients for yourself at conferences before, because one of the first questions I remember getting when I began teaching muscle testing classes was "Why would you train your competition?". Honestly, this had never occurred to me. As far as I can see, more people working in the holistic health field simply means more people hearing about what we do and the fact that it works. Even if you somehow have exactly the same training as someone else, you will attract different people and each of those people has a sphere of influence in turn that they are going to tell about the amazing session they just had, and so the news spreads. Now I am in the position where I train teachers and among instructors these belief systems are even more predominant; the idea that we need to be careful because if we train too many instructors then we won't have any more students. This is just silly. More instructors in our various modalities will lead to more students. We need to move past the either/or way of thinking as I mentioned in the earlier section about relationships. If we really believe that there is enough to go around and no need for competition, then we are not afraid to give away some of what we know. We can't say that we want to work cooperatively and then be afraid every time we meet another practitioner or instructor that they might be 'better' than us or that we don't really want them to be too successful in case they take something away from us. Walking the talk here means that we are willing to lend a helping hand, willing to say something good about our peers and willing to help people become better without fear.

Adam Grant's wonderful book 'Give and Take' brings this out beautifully for holistic practitioners. One of the things he mentions is the two-minute favour, which basically goes like this: if someone asks you for something and it's going to take you less than two minutes, you just do it. Immediately. No questions asked. What does this look like in real life? I just had one of these things come up. I received an email from someone asking an international organization that I work with if anyone knew an instructor for a particular holistic health class in Ontario. I didn't know off the top of my head, but I went into the Canadian Association's directory and scrolled through the listed instructors in Ontario to see if I could find anyone. When I didn't, I sent an email to the woman, telling her what I had done and that I hadn't had any luck, but then giving her the email address for the Canadian Association Board (I used to serve on this Board, so it was easy for me) and a few more ideas of places she could try. She wrote me back, saying that she had a couple more questions about different modalities and I answered them. They were simple questions; in writing both emails and looking through the directory I spent less than ten minutes. She replied thanking me profusely, saying that she had been sending out emails to so many people who wouldn't respond and that, "It has taken me weeks to get the information I needed." She is just getting started on her journey as a practitioner. For all I know, she might become intrinsic to the health and wellbeing of hundreds or thousands of people in the future. How terrible would it be if she had become so discouraged about not being able to find the information she was looking for that she gave up?

> If you're not breathing easily,
>
> if you are depleted beyond reason,
>
> you cannot hold up anyone else.
>
> Period.

On another level 'walking the talk' means taking care of our own health and wellbeing so that we can be clear channels to do good work for others. If you are tired, sick, or dealing with adrenal glands that are constantly on the verge of collapse, you are not able to do a good job with clients. If you are telling your clients that they need to be balanced or worked on once a month, that they need to take supplements, that they need to rest more, are you following that advice yourself? My husband has this wonderful/irritating habit of reminding me of this. Whenever I start making myself crazy by trying to do too many things at once or trying to push through rather than rest when I am unwell, he will ask "If you were your client, what would you tell you?" That the world will not fall apart if she takes a day off. That she can't write cheques from an empty bank account. That when a plane is in crisis, you need to put on your own oxygen mask first...

If you're not breathing easily, if you are depleted beyond reason, you cannot hold up anyone else. Period.

It can be easy for us to shove aside the idea of self-care as something that we don't have time for, especially if we aren't feeling too badly at the moment. After all, it never seems urgent (until it is, and then it's a problem). I think many of us were taught that sitting still or taking time out is a sign of laziness. It's not. If done properly, it is an investment in well-being. I think the problem is that we tend to have low-quality regeneration time. Watching TV in an exhausted heap at the end of the day or mindlessly scrolling a social media feed is not good quality rest time. The truth of the matter is that what is extremely restful and rejuvenating for one person feels exasperating to another, so the true question is; what do you need to do to refill? And remember that in order for this kind of a break to be impactful, it doesn't necessarily need to be long. There is evidence to suggest that some kind of cognitive break every hour helps you deal with complex problems more creatively and keeps you focused and sharp.

Years ago, when my twins were about four-years-old and an absolute handful, I had the opportunity to talk to Terry Willard, Master Herbalist, author and hero of mine at a health show. He was doing mini iridology readings and as I had just finished my iridology and herbology courses I was excited to see what he was going to come up with. He looked at my eyes, face and tongue for about a minute, then declared, "You have the problems of a frustrated artist." I was flustered – this was not what I had been expecting at all. I began to babble – I have two preschoolers and a job, I don't have time to draw or paint anymore, etc. He looked me in the eyes and said, "You only think you don't have time because you're a perfectionist. If you're a perfectionist, you think that everything you draw has to be perfect or you can't do it. Colour with your kids, play air guitar while you dance around, draw and throw it out, but do something, not caring how it turns out." That was our moment, and then it was the next person's turn.

I have had the chance to speak to him at greater length about a variety of health-topics since then, both in formal interviews and over a cup of tea, but it was that two-minute diagnosis that has stuck with me all these years. The message was clear; do the things that nourish your soul, be creative, take the time, and don't worry so much about what the result is.

For me to take an hour to doodle, to give myself an elaborate henna tattoo, to draw fantastic monsters with my little guy – these things leave my mind clearer and I find that the mental clutter seems to sort itself out a little as I engage this creative, right-side of my brain. Doing something physical can have the same effect, though depending on the individual this could range from going for a run to meandering slowly down the street window shopping. When I read articles that explain how everyone should run or everyone should meditate, or everyone should drink 3 cups of green tea in order to be calm and relaxed, I find myself getting frustrated. The whole basis of everything that we do in our work is that we are all unique and that our individual constitutions can not all be treated the same way. You, in all your weird and wonderful glory, need something different to feel joyful, rested and fulfilled than I do – so what makes your soul sing?

A few ideas, divided into two lists: first, things that can be done as quick cognitive breaks to help keep you joyful and inspired through your day, and second, things that can help restore on a deeper and more profound level:

Impromptu kitchen dance party

Doodling or colouring

Switch-on, zip up, tune in (if you are a Touch for Health practitioner, you know how to do this. If you aren't you can follow along with an old YouTube video of mine if you Google it)

A walk around the block

Playing with a pet

Deep rhythmic breathing for a full minute

Making a cup of tea and just drinking it calmly without doing anything else at the same time (except perhaps also eating a little dark chocolate...)

Playing/listening to music

Cuddling someone awesome

This is obviously not an extensive list, rather it is a jumping off point for you to come up with your own ideas for what allows you to take a quick cognitive break in the day and care for yourself. What you don't see on this list is "scroll Instagram". I am an avid social media marketer/communicator and I'm not saying that you shouldn't check your accounts, especially if this is one of the ways that you communicate with your clients. But please understand, this is not a break, this is work. This is not going to leave your mind and spirit refreshed and ready for your next client, this is going to burn you out. Leave the accounts for an allocated time and spend your break time doing something that transcends the cellphone.

Longer rests and habits:

Exchange sessions with a fellow practitioner, at least once a month ideally

Spend a day lost outside without any technology (garden, hiking, camping, beach, etc.)

Develop a daily exercise routine, consisting of whatever form of exercise you actually enjoy – the point here is not to 'shred' or lose weight, the point is to glory in your magnificent body's capacity of movement, so don't worry about what form is the best, think about what makes you happy

Read something that fascinates you

Make time for people who make you laugh

Many cultures and religions have an idea in them of a Sabbath, a day of rest when we not only are not expected to do any work, but where it would be frowned upon or even considered a sin to do so. In our hyperactive super-connected society, this has gone away. We have gained the convenience of always being able to reach anyone we want, but in turn, we are able to be reached by everyone all the time. The whole idea of 'office hours' has kind of disappeared. And yet, in order to truly relax and rejuvenate, it is important that you have some time dedicated to yourself and to your family where the outside world can't reach you. What that looks like in your world is up to you.

Action Plan:

1) How can you take care of yourself better? Create a short list of things that you want to add to your daily routine in order to rejuvenate yourself. When did you last have an appointment with another practitioner? If it has been longer than 6 weeks, go make one now (seriously, I'll wait).

_____

_____

_____

2) Look back through your calendar for the past few months. What activities caused the most joy and satisfaction? Can you take a moment now to schedule more of whatever causes you to feel great about your life?

3) What are you doing that would be contrary to the advice that you would give to one of your favourite clients? If anything at all comes to mind, make a list: these are the things that need to be changed. People are excellent at sniffing out hypocrisy. Walking the talk means that you will feel better and you will get better compliance from your clients too.

_____

_____

_____

4) Think about some of the work that you were doing in the last section, defining who you want to help and what issues you have built your soapbox on. Are there any aspects of your life that would contradict this bigger message? Is there anything that you can do outside of work that would be helpful, showing that you are walking your talk, even when there isn't a business-advantage to be had? Can you volunteer your services, your story or your experience? By making yourself available you also have the opportunity to be perceived as an expert in a niche and this can help you get the word out about your services as well as making a difference in the lives of those around you.

Some ideas:

_____

_____

_____

"I am authentic and transparent in my business."

"I choose to make self-care a priority."

RULE SEVEN: WALK THE TALK

-DAN 2017-

RULE # 8: SEEING IS BELIEVING

It's not real unless it's written down. There's a reason why so many of the Action Plan items throughout this little book have you writing things down and looking at examples rather than just thinking about them; writing things down, drawing them out, this makes them real in your brain in a different way. On a basic biochemical level your brain is wired to reward you for getting things done. Every time it seems like you are getting closer to a goal you get a sweet little hit of dopamine flowing through your brain. This would have helped our ancestors to keep moving towards a goal of food or shelter or creating something new and not give up, thus insuring our survival as a species. When we set actual goals and create plans and lists, we are rewarded every time we get a little closer. If you've ever written a To Do list for the day and put things on it that were ridiculously simple and didn't really need to be on there or worse, that you had already done, just for the joy of crossing them off, then you know the allure of the dopamine hit. It reinforces that you are on the right path, that you are making progress and helps you feel good about yourself in the meantime. The more definite the progress is, the more likely you are to get this good feeling, so progress that can be defined by crossing an item off a list, handing in an assignment or presenting something are much more rewarding to our brains and chemistry than simply mentally checking something off is. Write it down. This is one of the reasons behind creating a proper business plan as well, as we did in the first section.

I feel like I should add that 'write it down' has many forms. It could mean making a list, recording yourself so you can listen to or watch it later, drawing a picture, making a collage, etc. The point isn't necessarily to put it into words, the point is to create something tangible that can be checked in with over a period of time to make sure that you are on track. At the end of each day, you should be able to take stock mentally and ask yourself what you have done on that day that help move you toward your various goals. And this is not me advocating for you to work harder or never take a day off. It is totally possible for you to look back at the end of the day and say that what you did to move yourself forward was rest your mind in order to renew your problem-solving capabilities and play with your kids so that you are all happier and well-balanced. That is a good day.

When I first meet people and they hear about what I do for work and the fact that I home-school my kids and that we picked up and moved to the rainforest and that I make up songs for my chickens on a pretty regular basis; they usually tuck me squarely under the 'hippy-dippy quack' category in their brains. The truth of the matter is that I am almost obscenely organized. I have to be, it's not a matter of choice or temperament, it's a matter of survival. I have five-year plans broken down into what I need to do this year in order to be on track, broken down to what I need to do at different times in the year. At times when I have a lot going on in many different aspects of my life I might have a list of this month and this week and another list of the things that need to be done before a specific trip or class. Daily lists don't work as well for me, simply because with the sheer number of children and animals I am surrounded with I find that what I can get done on any individual day varies wildly, but you can usually figure out what needs to be done in a week and work with it accordingly.

Why am I telling you this? Because all too often I see people creating their vision boards, feeling great about them, sharing them on Instagram, rolling them up and then leaving them in a closet somewhere. I see people with lofty ambitions for the future but without a clear sense of how they are going to get there. Without a plan, goals are like New Year's Resolutions; they feel good to make because we get the little rush of being the kind of person that we would like to be, but it is temporary and doesn't affect any lasting change.

There is an interesting junction between what should be shared with others and what is better left unsaid here. There used to be the idea that it was a good thing for you to talk about your goals with people because you would feel a sense of obligation to follow through since you had people holding you accountable. Now however, we know that's not true. We care about status and how people perceive us, and it turns out that we get a little surge of dopamine when we talk to people about our goals too; it has to do with the sense of being the kind of person we want to be. When we say that we are going to volunteer for disaster relief, run a marathon, travel the world; we get to show someone that's the kind of person we are at heart and we bask a little in their admiration. But guess what? That premature basking comes with a price. Because we have already gotten their approval we are actually less likely to follow through. When you see people posting their Resolutions on Facebook and you click 'like'; understand that you are enabling them by giving them an underserved high and making it even less likely that they will do what they set out to do.

So how does this fit with all of the things I was saying before about being authentic and sharing your 'why'? It has to do with being clear about why you do what you do and being honest about what you are looking for in your business, but not putting information out there just for someone's approval. There must be a deeper reason. As you move towards your goals which you have clearly defined and created plans around, then, as you check things off, you can share them with the world and receive your congratulations, especially if meeting these goals helps you to achieve credibility in your field or on your soapbox.

The reason why I am going into this in such depth is because the world that we live in right now rewards us with little dopamine hits constantly without us doing much to earn them through our phones. Because every time you get a 'like' on your latest cat photo or a text message or an email we are receiving validation that we are special and important. This is why smartphones and social media can become so addictive; remember that dopamine is the same neurotransmitter that is released when we drink alcohol or coffee or gamble - dopamine is what makes those things

The trick is to understand the buzz for what it is, and not mistake it for the real thing.

addictive. If we allow ourselves to get into the habit of receiving our dopamine from activities that don't actually move us any closer to our goals, then we have less motivation to move ahead. So again, it's tricky, because in order to market effectively these days we need to be online, posting photos, generating shares and 'likes' and answering our emails; the trick is to understand the buzz for what it is, and not mistake it for the real thing.

The idea of a five-year-plan is what seems to work for me, but I understand that this is not for everyone_I like working with this kind of a time period because I tend to work with huge life-changing goals and it gives me space for unexpected emergencies, space to allow things to mature and come to fruition. It means that when your husband comes to you upset that certain things around your rainforest farm are not working out quite the way they were supposed to, you can say "it hasn't even been three years yet, we've got time, tranquilo."

Making things visual can help with the planning stages for your business as well. When you are thinking about how many sessions you would like to do in a week, or what your ideal schedule looks like; consider creating a mock schedule. Whatever construct you are using (or planning to use) to keep track of your clients; whether that is a paper day-timer, Google Calendar or some fancy App, fill in a week exactly the way you would like to see it. If you want to see clients 9-5, four days a week, then fill in mock appointments for those days. If you work with multiple modalities, write in exactly what you want to be doing in each of those spaces. For example, my favourite kind of day used to be five muscle-testing energy-work sessions with two massages thrown in. The massages gave my brain a bit of a break, the muscle testing sessions are easier on my body. Write it down exactly as you want to see the week unfold. Then make sure that this is placed somewhere you will see it often. If you are using something like Google Calendar, take a screen shot and put it on your desktop so you see it when you go to make appointments. It may sound gimmicky, but again, we are visual creatures and we respond to visual stimuli and goals.

Action Plan:

1) Create the prospective schedule (as mentioned above) mapping out exactly how many sessions of what kind, when. Be precise. This then becomes a visual goal, allowing you to align towards it. There is a sample for you to fill out on p.68.

2) Create a list of your goals. At this point, I'm not talking about a To Do list, I mean the big stuff that you want to tackle long-term in order to achieve what you want in your life. Depending on the way that your brain works, this might be a list of one, two, or five-year goals, but the point is to begin by dreaming big. Depending on how finicky you want to be at this point, you might have more than one list going. For example, I divide my lists into Professional, Personal and Farm. I understand that not everyone is attempting to raise goats, chickens and children in the jungle and therefore the categories are going to vary from person to person, but all I can offer here is my own experience! There is a huge amount of overlap between these of course, but it helps me to break it down in this way. Once you have your big goals down, break it down to this year – what needs to happen this year if you are going to meet your 5-year goals? Write it down. From there, you can create a

schedule by month and down to a weekly To Do list. It's not glamorous. It's a lot of work. But it gets results. Check in with your lists regularly and be realistic about how much you can achieve in what time period. If you are way ahead of your projected targets, dream bigger! If you're behind, either you aren't making great use of your time or you are being unrealistic with your expectations and might need to allow yourself a little more time (or reach out for help!).

Some BIG Goals:

_____
_____
_____
_____
_____
_____
_____
_____
_____
_____
_____
_____
_____
_____
_____
_____

3) Put a reminder of your big goals out somewhere where you will see it on a reasonably regular basis. When the going gets tough, and it will, these will help to remind you why you are doing what you do.

4) Look back at some of the notes in section two about creating the environment. Setting good habits makes it so much easier to achieve goals. Are there things on your list that can be broken down into small bits of daily effort? Create rituals around them by deliberately cultivating location and settings that will allow you to automate the process in your brain creating less cognitive stress.

"I clearly define my goals and objectives."

"I hold myself accountable to do my best."

RULE EIGHT: SEEING IS BELIEVING

PERFECT

SUNDAY 01	**MONDAY 02**	**TUESDAY 03**	**WEDNESDAY 04**
THURSDAY 05	**FRIDAY 06**	**SATURDAY 07**	**NOTES**

RULE #9: SEEK OUT OTHERS

Remember Rule Four: It's all about relationships. In that chapter we were discussing relationships between practitioners and from practitioners to clients and the importance of creating and nurturing these connections if we want to truly shine. This chapter is related to that, but slightly different; here, I am thinking much more about interacting with information than interacting with humans one-on-one. I will try to explain what I mean.

Every once and awhile on social media, I do a search – for words like 'kinesiology' or 'touch for health' and I see what comes up. If I find good content, I happily read it and share it. And often, I figure out who wrote it and begin following that person. This is how we expand our horizons and build networks of peers. It seems like such an easy thing to do and yet I am continually baffled by how few practitioners seem to do this. One morning while I was reading a health practitioner's blog, I mentioned this phenomenon to my husband. His reply was interesting. He has read some of the same kinds of business-books as I have. He said, all these people have been taught that content is king (see earlier section on marketing), that what they need to do is keep on creating content, just putting more and more of it out into the world, and that this will eventually grant them a following. Nowhere, he said, are people told to seek content out.

This is such a simple thought, but it had honestly never occurred to me. We are not told to go looking for content, just to continually produce it. But without looking for it, how would we know how we measure up? What information is already out there? How do we build bridges and make intuitive leaps and offer something that is different and evolving to the world? It can be easy to get locked into our own way of thinking. Reading and exploring the work of others within the same field offers us another point of view from within our world. (Remember the earlier suggestion for improving cognitive empathy?) Partly this is because the world of individually tailored news that we live in now supports and reinforces confirmation bias- meaning that we tend to only see more of what the internet knows we already believe and want to see. This can make it easy to start believing that everyone thinks the same way that you do and you don't see evidence to the contrary. We need to look outside of our own content, notice what other people are doing and especially notice

> *We need to look outside of our own content, notice what other people are doing and especially notice when they disagree.*

when they disagree.

This is closely related to some of the other concepts that we have already discussed; does it fit under the idea of marketing? Of Leveling Up? I honestly don't know, which is how it ended up as its own little section.

We should be consuming media in an intelligent way – not in the way of mindless social media scrolling, but in a way that involves seeking out the communities and thinkers that can help us to push ourselves further. This is true whether or not we agree with the other person's point of view. Remember that marketing has to be more of a conversation than it used to be in order to be effective. Our desire should be to reach out and communicate with others, not just to shout at them. This is the reason why you need to search out and pay attention to quality content – it is part of true communication. When you were putting together your avatar, one of the questions was about what kind of content your target individual is already consuming. If you make a point to look up some of these sources, it may help you to better understand your avatar's point of view.

This is a reminder that, while we do want to focus our marketing message on a select group of people, these are obviously not the only kind of people that we interact with. Believe it or not, I have actually had practitioners tell me that they don't want to be connected with me online because they don't want any of their followers to see my stuff. I understand not wanting to be connected with me based on my annoyingly-strange personality. I don't understand believing that you can basically censor the content available to your clients and students and that this would be a good thing. My guess would be that this comes from a sense of deep insecurity; a worry that you do not really know what you are talking about and that you will be 'found out' if people begin to look around. When we seek out others in our field and see what they have to say, we all become better. We can ask them for feedback, we can admit when we don't know something, we can challenge what they say and ask questions. This is a good thing.

We can extend this past just social media platforms; are you consistently reading and taking classes? This is closely linked to the material in the next section. We want to be upping our game. When I interview leaders within the holistic health industry for KinesioGeek Magazine, one of the last questions I ask them is what resources they would recommend, other than their own classes, books, whatever, for people who want to learn more about the subject. They don't usually come up empty handed. Those that we seek out as being the experts in the field? They know of other experts; they can point to other books, classes, podcasts, etc. as being wellsprings of information and they can do this ostensibly because they are doing research themselves. This is one of those times that you can act 'As if'. Think about what it is you want to be, how it is that you want to be seen, and then act 'as if' that is already true. When someone interviews you and asks this question, how are you going to respond?

Action Plan:

1) Do a search online within your favourite social-search-engine (Google, Twitter, Instagram, Pinterest, LinkedIn, Facebook, etc.) for keywords that you are interested in relating to your modality. Look at the individuals or companies that are putting a lot of content out into the world on the subject. What do you like about their message? Dislike? Do you agree? Can you make contact with them in some way; Following or Pinning or Friending or whatever so that you can keep tabs on them and what they are writing about?

2) Do a search online for information that directly contradicts what you believe about your field and read a little of it. Look at the arguments that are being put forward – is this a question of someone being misinformed? Is someone being vindictive? Can you see when they make a valid point? And if you find content where someone is being reasonable and you could engage them in conversation (not the people who are just name-calling and being nasty, we don't need to engage with the haters) can you offer your evidence?

"I am eager to learn from others in my field."

"I reach out and create connections."

RULE NINE: SEEK OUT OTHERS

-DAN 2017-

RULE #10: LEVEL UP

Complacency is death. Many associations already understand this, which is why they ask for Continuing Education Credits. I understand that not everyone is built with my need to be constantly devouring as much information as possible, nor should they be (apparently, I'm exhausting). But I do firmly believe that you should be taking stock every three months or so and noticing where you are at. This is not about competing with anyone, this is about being better than you were before. Leveling up can take different forms. It might involve taking another class within your chosen modality, or a class that would be considered complementary knowledge – for instance, taking a course in herbology when you are working as a massage therapist.

Does your field hold a yearly conference? That can be a fun way to hear about what is new, find interesting courses and meet people who are passionate about the same things you are. Many conferences also offer continuing education credits if you sign into the workshops and lectures that you attend. These also offer opportunities to build those important relationships and seek out more content.

Leveling up is not limited to just advancing in your field however. Upping your game as a practitioner might mean working on business and marketing skills or looking at your efficacy as a presenter. I read a lot of books about business and leadership, even though I would shudder to be described as a 'businessperson' first and foremost. Anything that you can do that makes you think in a different way is beneficial. You want to stretch your mind, force new connections in your neural net. Adding something novel and unexpected to your brain's daily tasks forces it to work harder, to slow down and think more deeply about things, rather than run on autopilot. When you read headlines that claim that doing crosswords, playing a musical instrument or having a pet can help to stave off dementia and Alzheimer's, this is the reason why. In Austin Kleon's book 'Steal Like an Artist' he talks about how his workspace is divided in two; the analog space (where no machines are allowed) and the digital space. The idea is that getting your hands into something, even if that is only in the form of writing things out the old-fashioned way with paper and a pen and maybe a few sticky notes, is more conducive to creativity than working in front of a screen. For most of us who work in the holistic health industry, we work with our hands all day, so we might not need this break in thinking as much as someone with an office job does. And yet, the theory is sound. The same principles apply in business. It can be easy for us to fall into ruts with our work. We are tired, we have a lot on the go, so we start doing the same things every day and don't really think about what could be improved upon. This is another reason why it can be helpful to attend conferences, conventions and trade shows; it gives you a chance to peek into everyone else's office and see what they are doing. Again, this isn't about competition – the purpose is not to see how others are doing and become discouraged or feel superior depending on what you are doing in comparison. It's about taking a moment to look from the outside in.

I have teenage kids and whenever I do something that my son thinks is particularly amazing (it happens rarely, but it happens) he uses this deep voice and says 'Level Up', usually accompanied by a 'pa-plink' sound that imitates coins or stars or something shiny being added to your character's score. When you are playing a game, getting a 'Level Up' is not when you quit; it's when the game becomes more interesting. You want to jump in and see where you have landed, what new bonuses or challenges can be found. If players were never able to progress through levels or unlock new challenges the game would become stagnant and boring very quickly and no-one would play. And yet, often we will spend years in a job without ever creating this kind of challenge for ourselves and not understand why we feel vaguely unsatisfied.

> When you are playing a game, getting a
> **'Level Up'**
> is not when you quit; it's when the game becomes more interesting.

Obviously, you already agree with this chapter and feel the need to Level Up in some way or, let's face it, you wouldn't be here (unless you are my mom, who is just reading this to be supportive. Hi mom!). I never would have dreamed that I could spend so long in a single industry. If you had told my high school self that I would fall so in love with a career path that I was determined to stay there forever, I would have laughed at you. And yet, here we are. And I am here still because of the daily changes and challenges that exist within this particular vocation. Every client is different, and I end up taking a different path with each person. Every group of students is different, so even though there is always a specific curriculum that needs to be followed in a class, the flow and the questions and the challenges that arise keep you on your toes. Leveling Up means always looking for a better way to serve our clients and this helps keep us from getting bored or complacent at the same time.

As you are probably painfully aware, the world is moving faster now than ever before in terms of information flow. You are probably within arms reach right now of a powerful computer that can answer any question for you, within seconds, if you simply type a few words or ask Siri. While it is impossible for us to keep up with everything all the time, you do want to make sure that you are searching for and reading enough new information that you are not falling behind. There is no shame in saying you don't know when someone bringing up some new modality or new research, but you don't want your answer to *always* be 'I don't know', or you will quickly lose that status as an expert in your field.

When I first began seeing muscle-testing clients, I had nothing but a couple of Touch for Health classes under my belt. I knew a fair bit about herbs and nutrition and 5-element theory from the other classes I had taken but was a muscle testing novice. I had the experience last year of speaking with a student who was feeling unsure about taking clients, thinking that she really didn't know enough to be seeing people in an office yet. I told her about when I began seeing clients and how I kind of cringe now, looking back at how inexperienced I was, to think that I was working on people with only that little bit of knowledge! Now, it happens that she was actually one of my first clients; she had brought her daughter who was about 2-years-old at the time in to see me for some digestive problems. In our conversation, she paused for a moment then said: "I remember that day with (my daughter) on the floor of your office. You changed our lives that day. I just want to bottle what you do and hold it." I was struck and humbled by that answer. No, I didn't know very much, but the little bit that I did know was enough that a little girl was able to heal herself and a mom was able to worry about her less, and that changed their lives. So there are two parts to the idea of Leveling Up – we want to constantly pursue excellence and become better, and at the same time not be afraid to go out and help people with exactly what we have to offer right now. Can you walk that line?

When Elon Musk was asked in an interview why he seems to be able to do things that other people view as impossible he gave an interesting answer. He said that he seeks out negative feedback and then acts on it and that this is an important step that many people overlook. We all like positive feedback right? It feels good to have people tell you what you are doing right, and yet, positive feedback does little to encourage growth. One of the tricky parts of teaching classes, particularly beginning levels of things, is balancing giving enough positive feedback that students don't become discouraged with negative feedback so they understand what they are doing incorrectly and can make changes before bad habits develop. A few thoughts about giving and receiving feedback: when offering feedback, we want to focus on 1) things that someone can change, and 2) the action, not the individual. Telling someone you don't like their voice when they are rehearsing a presentation is not helpful – they can do very little to change that. Mentioning that they sound a little monotonous and could modulate better is feedback that could be useful in improving. When we receive feedback, our first thought is often to justify or explain why

We don't have the same lens as you to see things through, so it looks different from over here.

we are doing it a certain why. Here's the thing – we know you have reasons for doing it like that. Of course you do. But we don't have the same lens as you to see things through, so it looks different from over here. Listen without justifying, and then you have the choice to decide how you want to use this information, either to make changes in the way you operate, or to forget it instantly and not worry about it again.

We can always be better. And yet, the most important things that we have are never going to be certificates or hours logged in classes; the ingredients most necessary for this work are always going to be love and clear intention. And this is not in any way an excuse for sloppy work or an excuse to not level up and become better with time. But it is a reminder that, if we are always approaching the work with these two things in mind, we are not going to do any harm.

Action Plan:

1) Find an industry event. Maybe it's not possible for you to go this year, but you can take a look at who the presenters are and what they are talking about. See if you can notice themes or industry trends. If websites are listed for the key presenters, you can look at their websites, read interesting posts and maybe get a feel for what they are doing and how you could implement some new ideas in your office with your clients.

Upcoming events in my industry:

_____

_____

2) Make plans to take two classes as soon as possible. The first should be related to your industry somehow, even if it is just a one-day workshop or auditing a class that you have taken previously. The second is designed to give your brain a refresh, so it can be in anything. This could be as simple as using a free app such as Duolingo to practice a new language everyday or as involved as signing up for a course as a local college. Paint, sing, learn proper bookkeeping, whatever is going to wake your mind up and inspire some creativity.

Things I'm excited to learn:

_____

_____

_____

3) Look at your business from the outside in. Create a perspective shift and try to imagine what your work would look like from someone else's point of view. What would they identify as strengths? Weaknesses?

Strengths:

_____

Weaknesses:

_____

4) Are you ever afraid to work on people thinking you don't know enough? What would help you to feel better equipped in those scenarios? Do you have a mentor that you can ask for help in this regard and who you trust to give you good feed-back?

I will feel equipped when:

_____

_____

_____

"I embrace growth and change."

"I use what I have at any given time,
to be the change I wish to see."

RULE TEN: LEVEL UP

IN CONCLUSION

Our industry is evolving. No longer do we live in a world where words like 'chakra' and 'acupressure' seem like exotic creatures that have no relevance in a modern age – most people have had some direct experience with alternative therapies by this point in time. They've seen Dr. Oz, they've purchased fish oil and probiotics. This makes our job both easier and more difficult. We no longer have the responsibility to introduce people to the realm of natural health, but we do often have to wade through a sea of misinformation in order to present them with viable information that can promote real change.

One of the issues that students often ask for help with is just the ability to explain what it is that we do properly. It's hard. So at the risk of upsetting anyone, the real question here is; do *you* understand what you do properly? Because, especially at the beginning, many of us simply know that we are working with energy and the body. We might toss around words like 'meridian', 'chakra' and 'intention' while discussing muscle testing, but you need to be really clear about what you actually mean. There are lots of ways to describe what it is that we do, from the extremely scientific (take a look at Dr. William Tiller's white pages for an example of how this can be done) to a very vague and idealistic concept. The words we use to describe what we do will change depending on the audience and the experience level of those we are speaking to. Make sure that it all fits.

This is where we tap in to that genuine voice that we were discussing earlier as well – don't try to be something that you're not here. But the ability to describe what we do and properly answer questions about muscle testing and how it works as a bio-feedback mechanism is one of the things that separates great practitioners from mediocre ones. Because of this, any time that you spend researching, reading and thinking about these systems is extremely valuable. When we make the decision to go from 'amateur' – someone who is interested in the work and has taken some classes, to 'professional' – someone who has thrown themselves into it and will now get it done, no matter what the cost; we also commit to having the best information to share with others. It's part of the package.

In this workbook, there is a lot of emphasis on understanding marketing, branding, leadership and customer service, but the truth is that none of these things will matter at all if you have not taken the time to polish your craft. As Steve Martin famously said when asked for advice, "Be so good they can't ignore you." When we are unequivocally good at what we do, we help to move the entire industry forward. Therefore, it is in our best interests to help each other to do exactly this – to explain who we are and what we do and to explain it clearly and beautifully enough that people understand and flock to it.

This is my wish for you.

Basic Business Plan: getting started

You can find Business Plan Templates online and work with them. Most of them are quite a bit more complicated than this one. I have tried to keep this as simple as possible and have annotated it slightly to assist as you think about the big questions facing a new business. Even if you have already been in business for awhile, it can help to go through this kind of procedure and take stock of where you are.

It is suggested that you work on this Plan as well as the Business Budget to give you a launching pad; you can work on it in pieces as you read the rest of the book.

And remember to have fun. You can change this, it can move and grow and evolve with you — it doesn't have to be high pressure. So charge forward!

And if you have no intention of putting in the effort to go through the whole thing, skip to the last question which, to my way of thinking, is the most important. It's not something that you will usually see on a business plan template, but if you can't answer this then it is going to be very difficult for you to succeed.

Business Name:

_____

Business Description (what do you actually do for people? This should be reasonably short and not get into the mechanics of the work):

_____
_____

Nature of the Industry (this blank is included in most templates, but for you will probably be something along the line of Holistic Therapy, or Bodywork — what are the terms used in your area?):

_____

Trends in the industry (look up the information specific to your region. Are more or less people looking for the kind of services you offer?):

_____
_____
_____
_____

Government Regulation (This varies from country to country and in Canada and the United States, even changes between provinces and states. In some areas, special licenses are required in order to be allowed to touch clients. In some areas, the terminology is regulated, and you can't use certain words. Do the research for your area. The key is that you want to know what you are getting into before you get started and not find out later that you are not in compliance with regulations and have to fix things.):

_____
_____
_____

Regulatory bodies (is there an association or regulatory board in your area that you need to be a member of?):

_____

Major Players (who is the 'competition' or the places where people are already getting some of their needs met? Remember that this might be other practitioners, but also might be other institutions and industries; for example, if you are trying to teach people to be more responsible for their health, the local walk-in clinic might be a major player.):

_____
_____
_____
_____
_____

Sub-question (not something you will usually see in a business plan): What are the status quos in your industry? The assumptions that everyone makes as to how things are done and how they must continue to be done?

_____
_____
_____
_____
_____

Market Segment (what is your niche? Who are you going to serve? At this point, you can just put in a short version, but check out the sections about creating your avatar in the Marketing chapter):

_____
_____

Products and/or services (here is where you get into more detail about what you do. List the kinds of products and services you offer and maybe think about the percentage of your total business that belongs to each.):

_____
_____
_____
_____
_____

Pricing (look at the notes in the first chapter about pricing and come up with a set of numbers that feels right to you):

_____

Competitor's strengths and weaknesses, competitive advantage (here is where you want to list what others are doing well and poorly in your area and how you intend on capturing some market share. Remember that competing in this case doesn't always mean being able to do everything better than everyone else; what it means is figuring out what you do best and capitalizing on that.)

_____
_____
_____
_____
_____

Marketing and Promotion (have you considered some favourite strategies from the section on Marketing? Do you have a monthly budget that you can assign to this?

_____
_____
_____
_____

Hours of operation:

_____

Employees (do you need to hire? How many people? Have you created a hiring policy and job description?):

_____

_____
_____
_____
_____

Most Importantly: What is the change that you are seeking to make? What are you going to do that is different and how is it going to be better for those you wish to serve? How will you know that you have succeeded?

_____
_____
_____
_____
_____
_____

Proposed Budget

Most things, you can start small with and increase over time as your income increases, but some expenses, you are going to have right from the beginning and you don't want the little things to add up and take you unawares. This is a guide, designed so that you can begin thinking about what your operating expenses might look like. This is by no means complete; if you purchase book-keeping software it will have categories in place that will let you see more easily what expenses might be expected.

Income projection (Figure out how many sessions you want to be doing in a month and what you are going to charge for each session. Be realistic in your projections, understanding that it might take awhile for you to build up your client base to the number that you want.):

Operating costs – Let's look at monthly expenses to start:

Rent/mortgage:_____

Utilities (remember to include phone and internet):_____

Office supplies (paper, pens, things that are used up on a daily basis):_____

Consumable supplies (massage oil, sheets, tea, whatever gets used up over the course of normal sesions):_____

Employee wages and benefits if applicable:_____

Association memberships:_____

Insurance:_____

Marketing and promotion:_____

Fees for processing payments (credit cards, PayPal, etc.)_____

One-time expenses:

Renovation costs:_____

Office furnishings (chairs? Massage tables? Desk?): _____

Office equipment (computer, printer, etc.):_____

Any special equipment needed for the work:_____

Things you don't usually see in budgets that I want to include:

Conference and continuing education fund – throughout this book, the benefits of leveling up, attending conferences with your peers, taking more courses, etc. have been emphasized. If you can set aside a small amount every month than there is always a little on hand to make these things more attainable. If you don't do this, it's easy to think 'oh I can't afford it,' when opportunities present themselves. Put the money aside and then make yourself spend it on your education, in whatever form makes the most sense for you at this point in time, before the end of the year. You won't regret it.

_____

Good Deeds fund: a little money put aside every month that then allows you to give to a local charity or a cause that you feel strongly about. Even if this is a small amount, it can help you reconnect with your reasons Why you do what you do. Generosity is good marketing as it helps people to have a positive feeling about you, your brand and your impact on the community. And it adds a few karma points in your favour, and that can't possibly be a bad thing.

_____

At the end of the month, you compare the actual numbers against your projections. At this point, you can make changes in your projections or in your spending, whichever makes more sense.

Appendix A: Classes and information

Touch for Health: considered the foundation of SK work. Four levels, 15 hours each to learn the fundamentals of how to muscle monitor, the association between specific muscles, and meridians of energy flow and how to give a great balance.

www.gemskinesiology.com: shameless plug for my own website, but the reason is sound – this is the home of KinesioGeek Magazine which is, as far as I am aware at this time, our one-and-only industry journal. And it's free! And it includes work from writers all over the world... I could go on, but I won't, just go check it out.

GEMS Classes: Designed to help students go from basic knowledge of techniques taught in Touch for Health to being confident practitioners. GEMS Flow works with a flow chart and scan sheets to break students out of the boxes that balancing techniques are traditionally taught in. GEMS Business goes over much of the same material as is seen in this workbook, helping holistic practitioners create the business of their dreams. GEMS Nutrition provides the basics of nutrition alongside 5-element scan sheets that can be added into the protocols already in use from GEMS Flow. More information about each of these classes in available on the website www.gemskinesiology.com

Appendix B: Recommended Reading & References

Give and Take, *Adam Grant,* 2013: About the 2 minute favour as well as promoting the concept of generosity and cooperation as ways of moving ahead in your industry, whatever that may be.

Steal Like an Artist, *Austin Kleon*, Workman Publishing Company, 2012: I stole (like an artist) the idea of creating dual workspace; analog and digital, from this book. This is perfect for helping you tune the idea of innovating and changing what already exists in the world to something with your own unique stamp on it.

Linchpin, *Seth Godin*, Portfolio/Penguin, 2010: What's a linchpin? It's something indispensable. And as we set out to be more than just cogs-in-the-machine, this book offers some guidance on that and how to tap into your potential.

This is Marketing, *Seth Godin*, Portfolio/Penguin 2018: probably the best overview of permission-based marketing available and enjoyable to read.

The Art of Possibility, *Rosamund Stone Zander and Benjamin Zander*, Penguin Books, 2000: For helping you to flip your point of view, changing what is to what could be. There are shorthand rules that are easy to remember that will change the way you see yourself and your work.

The War of Art, *Steven Pressfield*, Black Irish Entertainment, 2002: Getting over your own resistance to be able to then do something truly great. I especially recommend this for the advice and insight on becoming a professional, and what that means.

Leaders Eat Last, *Simon Sinek*, Portfolio, 2014: Because leaders are not here to bully, they are here to serve.

Start with Why, *Simon Sinek,* Portfolio, 2011: Because if you don't really truly understand why you are doing things, there is no point. Because this is how we win over hearts and minds – by connecting with someone's why.

Personal Branding for Dummies, *Susan Chritton*, John Wiley and Sons Inc. 2014: To help you understand better what 'brand' can entail and how to go about getting started if you feel like you need a more step-by-step approach than is offered in this workbook .

Kidd, D.C. & Castano, E. (2013). Reading literary fiction improves Theory of Mind. *Science*, 342, 377-380.

William Tiller, Institute for Psychoenergetic Sciences, white pages, www.tillerinstitute.com

A KinesioGeek Manifesto

I will use what I know to create balance in the world around me.
Understanding that sometimes, in order to be balanced with
those I love, I need to step back and take care of myself.

I strive to learn every day. I feed my logic brain lots of physiology,
physics and nutritional facts and my gestalt brain with
music, chocolate and art.

I see the others on my path as teammates and friends and
understand that the easiest way for me to achieve my goals in the
world is to help them get there too, not to try to cut them down.

I remember that most of what we know for a fact today will be
dis-proven and changed in the next 100 years,
so I don't take myself too seriously.

I pay respect to those who came before me, remembering that we
can only do what we do because we stand on the shoulders of
giants. I am respectful enough of these heroes to not let
innovation end with them, but to take up the torch
and run-like-hell with it.

I use Specialized Kinesiology to be the best version of myself and
to help you to do the same.
Letting the you at the center shine through.

Appendix 3: Core Value Words

Acceptance
Accessibility
Accomplishment
Accountability
Accuracy
Achievement
Activity
Adaptability
Adventure
Affection
Affective
Aggressive
Agility
Alert
Altruism
Ambition
Amusement
Anticipation
Appreciation
Approachability
Assertiveness
Attentive
Availability
Awareness
Balance
Beauty
Being the Best
Belonging
Best
Bold
Bravery
Brilliance

Calm
Candor
Capable
Careful
Caring
Certainty
Challenge
Change
Character
Charity
Cheerful
Citizenship
Clean
Clear
Clever
Collaboration
Comfort
Commitment
Common Sense
Communication
Community
Compassion
Competence
Competency
Competitive
Completion
Composure
Comprehensive
Concentration
Confidence
Confidential
Conformity

Connection
Consciousness
Consistency
Content
Continuity
Contribution
Control
Conviction
Cooperation
Coordination
Cordiality
Correct
Courage
Courtesy
Craftiness
Craftsmanship
Creation
Creative
Credibility
Cunning
Curiosity
Customer Focus
Customer Satisfaction
Customer Service
Daring
Decency
Decisive
Dedication
Delight
Democratic
Dependability
Depth

Determination	Enthusiasm	Focus
Development	Entrepreneurship	Foresight
Devotion	Environment	Formal
Devout	Equality	Fortitude
Different	Equitable	Freedom
Dignity	Ethical	Fresh
Diligence	Excellence	Friendly
Direct	Exciting	Frugality
Discipline	Exhilarating	Fun
Discovery	Exuberance	Generosity
Discretion	Experience	Genius
Diversity	Expertise	Giving
Dominance	Exploration	Global
Down-to-Earth	Explore	Goodness
Dreaming	Expressive	Goodwill
Drive	Extrovert	Gratitude
Duty	Fairness	Greatness
Eagerness	Faith	Growth
Ease of Use	Faithfulness	Guidance
Economy	Family	Happiness
Education	Famous	Hard Work
Effective	Fashion	Harmony
Efficient	Fast	Health
Elegance	Fearless	Heart
Empathy	Ferocious	Helpful
Empower	Fidelity	Heroism
Encouragement	Fierce	History
Endurance	Firm	Holiness
Energy	Fitness	Honesty
Engagement	Flair	Honor
Enjoyment	Flexibility	Hope
Entertainment	Fluency	Hospitality

Humble
Humility
Humor
Hygiene
Imagination
Impact
Impartial
Impious
Improvement
Independence
Individuality
Industry
Informal
Innovative
Inquisitive
Insight
Inspiration
Integrity
Intelligence
Intensity
International
Intuition
Invention
Investing
Inviting
Irreverence
Joy
Justice
Kindness
Knowledge
Leadership
Learning

Level-Headed
Liberty
Listening
Lively
Local
Logic
Longevity
Love
Loyalty
Mastery
Maturity
Maximizing
Meaning
Meekness
Mellow
Members
Merit
Meritocracy
Meticulous
Mindful
Moderation
Modesty
Motivation
Mystery
Neatness
Nerve
No Bureaucracy
Obedience
Open-Minded
Openness
Optimism
Order

Organization
Originality
Outrageous
Partnership
Passion
Patience
Patients
Patriotism
Peace
People
Perception
Perfection
Performance
Perseverance
Persistence
Personal Development
Personal Growth
Persuasive
Philanthropy
Playfulness
Pleasantness
Poise
Polish
Popularity
Positive
Potency
Potential
Powerful
Practical
Pragmatic
Precision
Prepared

Preservation
Pride
Privacy
Proactive
Productivity
Profane
Professionalism
Profitability
Progress
Prosperity
Prudence
Punctuality
Purity
Pursuit
Quality
Rational
Real
Realistic
Reason
Recognition
Recreation
Refined
Reflection
Relationships
Relaxation
Reliable
Resilience
Resolute
Resolve
Resourceful
Respect
Responsibility

Responsiveness
Rest
Restraint
Results
Reverence
Rigor
Risk
Sacrifice
Safety
Sanitary
Satisfaction
Security
Self Awareness
Self Motivation
Self Responsibility
Self-Control
Self-Directed
Selfless
Self-Reliance
Sense of Humor
Sensitivity
Serenity
Serious
Service
Shared Prosperity
Sharing
Shrewd
Significance
Silence
Silliness
Simplicity
Sincerity

Skill
Smart
Solitude
Speed
Spirit
Spirituality
Spontaneous
Stability
Standardization
Status
Stealth
Stewardship
Strength
Structure
Success
Support
Surprise
Sustainability
Sympathy
Synergy
Systemization
Talent
Teamwork
Temperance
Thankful
Thorough
Thoughtful
Timely
Tolerance
Tough
Traditional
Training

Tranquility
Transparency
Trust
Trustworthy
Truth
Understanding
Unflappable
Unique
Unity
Universal
Useful
Utility
Valor
Value
Value Creation
Variety
Victorious
Vigor
Virtue
Vision
Vitality
Warmth
Watchful
Wealth
Welcoming
Willfulness
Winning
Wisdom
Wonder
Worldwide
Work/Life Balance

Acknowledgements:

Thank you to my family; Aidan (love of my life, Super Nerd, proof-reader who reminds me that not everyone can read my mind), Ezra and Hannah (Touch For Health Geniuses, show-tune singers, poser of hypothetical situations that can only be solved by discussing the alignment of fictional characters), and Jorah (jungle wild-child, half dolphin, artist). Being insanely driven is not the most attractive quality or the easiest to live with and they somehow manage it anyways.

Thank you to the Energy-Working-Muscle-Testing-Family around the world: instructors, students, practitioners, all of us working together to try to change the world in the best possible way. We can do this. Thank you to the clients who trust me to be part of their journey.

I hope you found something helpful here. Thanks for coming on this adventure with me.

www.ingramcontent.com/pod-product-compliance
Lightning Source LLC
Chambersburg PA
CBHW041722210326
41598CB00007B/745